A CAMBRIDGE TOPIC BOOK

The Viking Ships

Ian Atkinson

Published in cooperation with Cambridge University Press
Lerner Publications Company, Minneapolis

Editors' Note: In preparing this edition of *The Cambridge Topic Books* for publication, the editors have made only a few minor changes in the original material. In some isolated cases, British spelling and usage were altered in order to avoid possible confusion for our readers. Whenever necessary, information was added to clarify references to people, places, and events in British history. An index was also provided in each volume.

LIBRARY OF CONGRESS CATALOGING IN PUBLICATION DATA

Atkinson, Ian, 1936—
  The Viking ships.

    (A Cambridge topic book)
    Includes index.
    SUMMARY: Discusses the construction and uses of different types of Viking ships.

    1. Viking ships—Juvenile literature. [1. Vikings. 2. Ships]
I. Title.

VM17.A84   1980   623.8'21   80-11690
ISBN 0-8225-1221-1   lib. bdg.

6/81 NEMBF—5.95/n4

This edition first published 1980 by Lerner Publications Company by permission of Cambridge University Press.

Original edition copyright © 1979 by Cambridge University Press as part of *The Cambridge Introduction to the History of Mankind: Topic Book.*

International Standard Book Number: 0-8225-1221-1
Library of Congress Catalog Card Number: 80-11690

Manufactured in the United States of America.

This edition is available exclusively from:
Lerner Publications Company, 241 First Avenue North, Minneapolis, Minnesota 55401

1 2 3 4 5 6 7 8 9 10 85 84 83 82 81 80

Contents

1 To the furthest west

Eric the Red was a young Viking. He and his father were outlawed in Norway for some killings. They lived in Iceland for several years and Eric got married there after his father died. One day, Eric's slaves killed a farmer by causing a landslide to fall onto his farm. A kinsman of the farmer chased the slaves and killed them, whereupon Eric killed the kinsman and his companion. Eric had to make a quick escape from the relatives of the dead men but he returned later to collect the roofposts of his house. These were held by a man called Thorgest who would not give them up. In the fight that followed, Thorgest lost two of his sons and some of his servants.

The Icelanders found Eric guilty of manslaughter and he was outlawed for three years. This meant that he could be killed on the spot if he was found in the country during that time. He had therefore to sail away overseas – but where to? If he went east, he would land in Norway where he was already an outlaw. A southerly course would lead him to the islands off Scotland and Ireland which were well populated with Norwegians, and his welcome would probably be unpleasant. Northwards, a short voyage would bring a ship to Arctic ice. So Eric went to the little-known and un-named land to the west of Iceland.

He stayed there for three years and explored the land to find the richest soil. He claimed land along a fiord that he called Ericsfiord, before he returned to Iceland to find other men who would be willing to settle in this new land. Because he wanted to persuade people to go there, he called his new land Greenland, although much of it was covered with ice and snow. Still, the very best land in Greenland was better than some of the land that was then being farmed in Iceland. Some men agreed to join him and, in the spring of the year 986, they sailed with their families, servants and belongings in twenty-five ships. There was a terrible gale and some ships turned back. Only fourteen ships reached Greenland to start a colony of perhaps three hundred people.

Among these people was a man called Heriolf whose son was away in Norway at that time. The son, Biarni Heriolfsson, returned to Iceland that summer to find that his father had left. He decided to join his father and was told the sea route to follow but he was blown off course. The land that he first sighted was well forested and had low hills. He knew that this was not Greenland so he turned north and sailed for two days along the coast. Then he came upon a second land, flat and densely wooded, which he realised was not Greenland either. After that he lost sight of land for three days until he came to a barren land of ice and rock. He turned away from this land and sailed for four days until he reached his father's house in Greenland.

It is obvious from this Icelandic story that Biarni had found the east coast of North America by accident. The Greenlanders were too busy building their new homes to follow up this discovery at once but they had a great need of timber. So some years later Eric the Red's son, Leif, asked Biarni about his voyage and then bought his ship. Leif back-tracked on Biarni's

A stone arrowhead made by American Indians in North America, but found by archaeologists in a Viking graveyard in Greenland. The spindle whorl, (diameter about 4 cm, 1.5 in.) of the kind used by Viking women, was found at L'Anse-aux-Meadows in Newfoundland. So people seem to have carried goods in both directions.

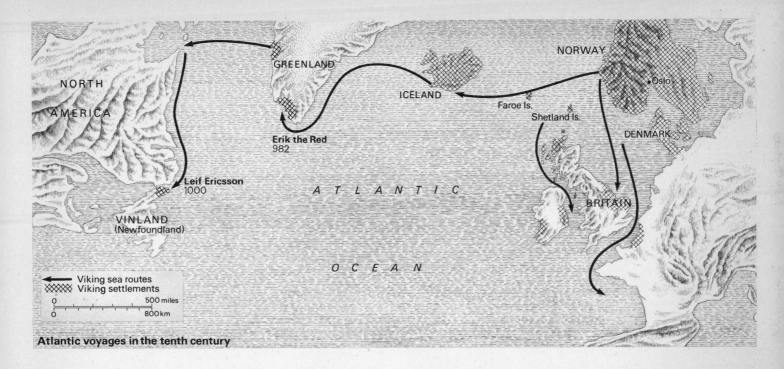

Atlantic voyages in the tenth century

course and explored the coast of the country which we now call Canada. He sailed south until he found a place where he could stay for the winter. In the spring, he returned to Ericsfiord with a valuable cargo of timber and with some wonderful stories. He called the place Vinland because he claimed to have found grapes growing there.

Leif's brother, Thorvald, was the next person to explore the coast but he was killed by a native arrow. This did not deter their sister and her husband from taking about sixty men, some with their wives, to found a colony in Vinland where the grapes grew. This colony lasted for three years by fishing, farming and trading with the natives whom the Vikings called Skraelings (Weaklings). Eventually, the Skraelings became unfriendly and the Vikings were outnumbered, so they returned to Greenland. After this, the Greenlanders continued to sail to the nearest forests of Canada for timber, but there is no other record of Europeans sailing to America until the time of Columbus.

Some people have doubted the truth of these stories, which are part of the great body of literature known as the Icelandic *sagas*. Written during the twelfth and thirteenth centuries, the sagas are one of our major sources of information about the Viking period. The account that they give of the Viking settlement in Vinland was written long before the European voyages of exploration in the sixteenth century and yet the geographical details are quite accurate. Recently, remains of Viking-type houses have been found in Newfoundland and an American Indian arrowhead has been found in Greenland. These and other finds have been scientifically dated to about the year 1000. But arguments continue, for example, about the grapes. Grapes do not now grow as far north as Newfoundland. However, people do gather squashberries in that area; they look rather like small grapes and a wine can be made from them. Whether this is the true explanation of the wine or not, it is now safe to say that Viking ships were the earliest ships known to have crossed the Atlantic and explored part of the coast of North America.

2 Finding a way over the sea

Although the shortest distance between the coasts of Norway and Greenland is about 1,500 kilometres (900 miles), the Vikings preferred to take a longer route, south of Iceland, and thereby avoid pack ice. The did not always call at Iceland and so their voyage could be well over 1,600 kilometres (1,000 miles). The crews must have had great confidence in their pilots. But these pilots did not have a compass to show them the direction they had to take and they did not have instruments to tell them how far east or west they had sailed.

Early sailors probably hardly ever lost sight of land, making their way around coasts or from island to island. Obviously, this makes a voyage much longer than one which crosses the sea in a straight line. So men began to take the risk of losing their way on the open sea. An experienced pilot may have known how far north or south he was from his home by noting the position of the Pole Star at his home. He could use an upright notched stick or his mast to look past at the star and note how far up the upright the star appeared. Later, at sea, he would be on the same latitude if the star was seen against the same mark. A higher

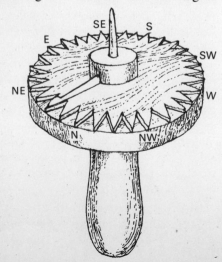

Viking sailors may have used a bearing dial like this to check their direction against sun and stars. The drawing is based on a small fragment found in Greenland. The dial is about 7 cm (nearly 3 in.) in diameter.

notch meant that the ship was at a higher latitude nearer the North Pole. On land, this method could show latitude to within twenty-four kilometres (fifteen miles) and, at sea, a ship that was only this distance off course would be within sight of its destination in normal conditions of visibility. But, how accurately could one assess the height of the star on a rolling sea?

The sun's position could also be noted, but it moves across the sky throughout the day and its position in the sky alters slightly every day. This makes it much more difficult to use accurately, especially when the sailor does not have a clock to tell him when it is precisely midday. The Vikings must have used the sun, however, because the Pole Star would sometimes be hidden by cloud and, in the Arctic, it would not be visible at midsummer because of the constant daylight. In the tenth century, an Icelander called Oddi produced latitude tables for certain stars including the sun. He was then nicknamed Star-Oddi.

There are times when cloud covers the sky for days on end especially in the areas where the Vikings sailed. When this happens it is easy to lose all sense of direction and drift around and be carried by ocean currents until the sailors are hundreds of miles from where they think they are. To overcome this problem, other methods had to be tried. Floki Vilgerdarsson was an early Viking explorer of Iceland who did not know the exact course to sail from the Faroe Islands. So he took some ravens with him. These are land birds and they are black and therefore can be easily seen against the light sky. He released the first bird the day after the islands were lost from view. It soared high and saw the islands and flew back to them. Later, the second bird was released and it also soared high but saw nothing and landed back on the mast. The next day, the third bird flew forward over the horizon and Floki sailed after it. He found the land which he named Iceland. His friends nicknamed him Raven-Floki.

Once a ship had sailed over a route, then the pilot could give instructions and directions to other pilots and there would be no need to carry birds. Biarni Heriolfsson knew when he reached a land of forests that he was not at Greenland. Although he was off course, his instructions were good enough to allow him to find his way over 800 kilometres (500 miles) of strange sea to a land which he had never visited before. He, in his turn, was able to give Leif Ericsson good directions so that the Greenlanders could go to the strange land for timber.

Such instructions described very clearly the landmarks that one would see first when approaching the new land, and the latitude on which they would be found. Such a landmark would often be the highest mountain on a coast. So the instructions for the voyage from Iceland to Greenland would tell the sailor to go from Snaefell (Snowhill) in Iceland, which is the clearest landmark on that part of the coast and therefore takes the longest time to disappear below the horizon. Then they would give the direction to sail in order to catch sight of Blaserk (Blackshirt) which is a 3,500-metre (11,500-ft) mountain in Greenland. With such good landmarks as these, the sailor would be told that he would be out of sight of land for one day. The instructions would then describe the main landmarks on the voyage round the Greenland coast to the settlements.

The number of days that one would be out of sight of land would depend on the weather conditions. The wind was important, but the visibility was more important still. Vikings would wait for clear weather rather than for a favourable wind. The Iceland–Greenland voyage is 560 kilometres (350 miles), which would be nightmare in fog. But in clear weather, one can sail 160 kilometres (100 miles) before losing sight of the peak of Snaefell and be more than 160 kilometres (100 miles) from Greenland when Blaserk comes into view. In the very clear Arctic light it is sometimes possible to become aware of one mountain before one has lost sight of the other.

Even when out of sight of land an experienced sailor could find information. As there are landmarks on land, so there are seamarks on the ocean. Whales gathered in large numbers to feed at an area which was half a day's sail south of Iceland. Birds, as we have seen, could indicate the direction of land, but the sailor could not always be sure when he saw a seabird if it was heading towards or away from land. Migrating birds on their annual flights did give a clear indication, because they always followed the same route; geese flying between Britain and Iceland were of particular use to the Vikings.

A very experienced helmsman, once his course had been set, could keep to that course by watching the direction from which the wind was blowing and from which the swell was running. If the wind changed direction, the motion of the sea would follow it, but more slowly. A clever man would notice this change and allow for it. A not-so-clever helmsman would steer according to the direction of the waves and, as the swell changed direction, he would change course without realising it. This of course could more easily happen when the sky was covered with cloud.

It is just possible that there was a device for finding direction even on a very overcast day. In the thirteenth century, Icelanders had a stone which they called a sun-stone. This was probably calcite which, when held up to the light, changes colour. On a cloudy day one can turn round until one finds the direction in which the sun polarises the light and one knows that that is where the sun is to be found. This stone can be found on an island in Oslofiord and, according to the sagas, a similar stone was used by a Viking king in the eleventh century. But, at the moment, there is no way of proving that this story is true.

With experience, then, and careful observation, and perhaps a simple instrument or two, a Viking pilot was able to navigate reasonably well over wide stretches of sea, in normal conditions. But things could go wrong. Even a famous sailor like Eric the Red once got badly lost. After his son Leif had been to Vinland, he himself set sail for it, but he ran into a storm on the day when he expected to sight the new country. The ship was blown far out to sea and, unknown to Eric, there was a strong current driving him out faster. After the storm he sailed westwards for some days but failed to find any land at all. He was lost and he tried to go home to Greenland but, being farther out in the ocean than he expected to be, he was heading northwards to nowhere and the current that he did not know about was still taking the ship towards the centre of the ocean. Luckily, just as the Vikings were about to give up hope, they spotted an Irish seabird and realised that they were much farther away from Greenland than they had estimated. They then sailed north until they were at the same latitude as Iceland, and next turned westwards until they sighted it. Once they knew where they were, it was easy to get back to Greenland, but they had been away for most of the summer, and were worn out.

This voyage tells us much about Viking navigation. It also tells us that they had ships they could trust to ride the North Atlantic.

3 The Gokstad ship

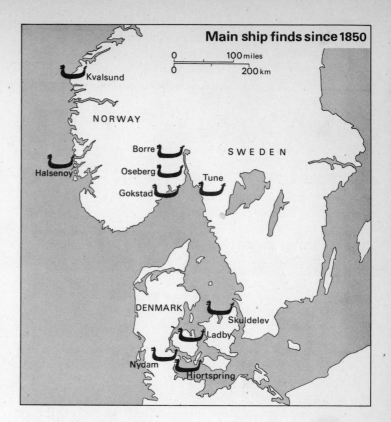

Main ship finds since 1850

What sort of ships were capable of making such voyages? A hundred years ago it was known that the Vikings had wooden ships with one square sail on a central mast, and that these ships could be rowed. These facts were mentioned in so many writings that they could not be wrong, but everything else was open to argument. Sources of information were not really very helpful. The sagas had been written down centuries after the voyages, and anyway they did not give descriptions of the ships, only references. European and Arab chroniclers who did write when the Vikings were sailing, trading and raiding were more concerned with Viking behaviour than the technical details of the ships. As for pictures, it was usually difficult to know what the artist was trying to show.

Today we know a great deal about those ships, and we owe our knowledge to the fact that for most of their history the Vikings were pagan. It was their custom to be buried or cremated with the goods that they would need in the next world. These goods could include arms, furniture and even a ship if the Viking was rich enough (though sometimes the ship may in fact have been worn out). The body and the goods were loaded on board and often the friends of the dead person threw on blazing wood to turn it into a cremation pyre. Apart from a few nails, that sort of funeral left little of the ship. But burial was a different matter.

Buried ships were placed in deep holes, but there was usually also a sizeable mound of earth visible above ground. Many such mounds are to be found in southern Norway where local people have always called them royal graves. One ship was unearthed in the eighteenth century, though nothing of what was found has been preserved. Another ship was discovered by local farmers at Borre as they made a new road in 1850, and this time some of the goods found in it reached museums where it was realised that there might be more to come from other mounds. The next important discovery was at Tune in 1867. Here, at last, some of the ship's timber was preserved for study and archaeologists

began to learn something of how the Vikings wrought the wood for their ships.

So far the discoveries had been quite interesting to scholars, but not very important. Then, in 1880, the discovery was made that caught the imagination of millions. A Viking ship, dating from about AD 900, was found at Gokstad. Some of the upper parts of the stem and stern, which had been nearer the surface, had rotted away, and the mast had probably been cut so as not to protrude above the surface of the mound. Otherwise the ship was complete.

A certain amount of damage had been done to the ship. The mound had been disturbed by intruders who had smashed their way into the side of the ship, apparently long ago, to get to the body. They may have thought that they were being haunted by the ghost of the man in the mound, or that the mound-dweller was bringing bad luck to the neighbourhood. Whatever the motive, it is quite likely that some of the goods had been stolen, but the mound breakers had left seven beds, woollen and silk textiles, horse harnesses (some ornamental and expensive), and also the verge boards of a tent and a wooden board game. In another part of the ship were found kitchen utensils, including a cauldron, a wooden cask which was probably for water, chopping boards, two wooden plates and smaller utensils. The dead man had been accompanied by the skeletons of twelve horses, six dogs and a peacock, which must have been a rarity in Scandinavia. There were also three rowing boats.

The ship had been damaged by the weight of the rocks and soil that had been piled on it during burial. However, the clay in which it had been buried had preserved the ship because it was airtight. The timbers would soon have rotted after they had been exposed to the air, but the excavators understood this and knew how to treat them.

The Gokstad ship is just over 23 metres (76 ft) long and the maximum width is 5.2 metres (17 ft); the height from the bottom of the keel to the gunwale amidships is 2 metres (7 ft). The weight of the hull fully equipped is estimated at 20 tonnes. It contained a strong mast fish (support) and 16 pairs of oars.

The ship being uncovered at Gokstad in 1880.

The interior of the Gokstad ship as it may have appeared, looking towards the stern. The loose deck planks have been left out.

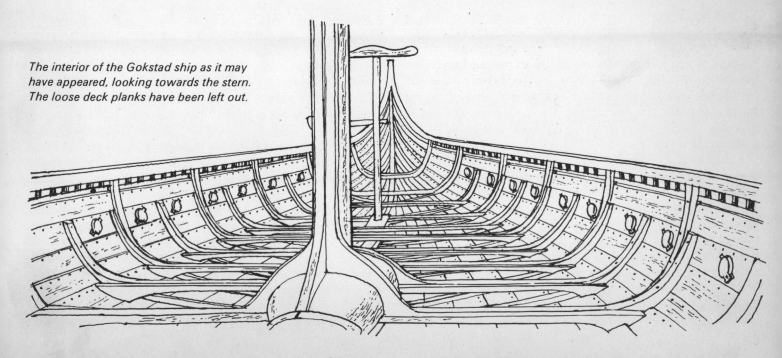

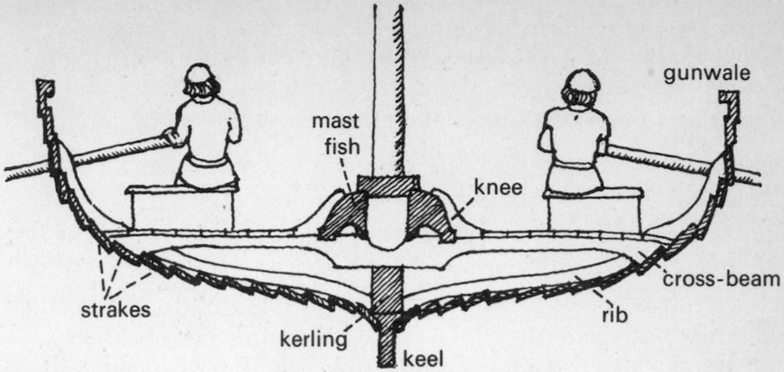

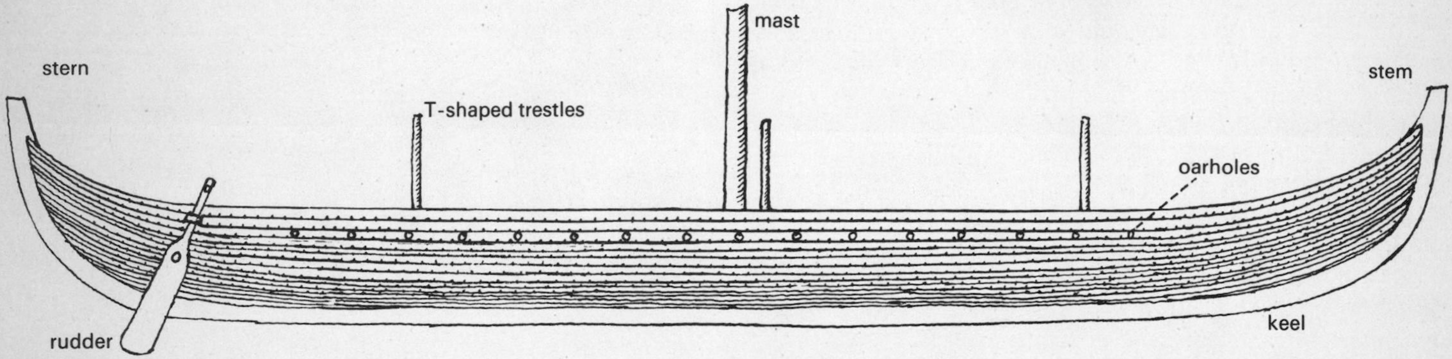

The Gokstad ship. The cross-section amidships shows rowers sitting on boxes, though it has been suggested that they may have stood. Note how the keel is shaped to give a watertight join with the first strakes. The T-shaped trestles shown in the side view of the ship, below, were probably used to support the yard, sail and, possibly, the mast when the ship was being rowed.

It is a strong ship because it was built on a solid, heavy keel which had been taken from a straight oak tree which must have been about 25 metres (80 ft) high. Such trees can no longer be found in Norway.

The keel, the ship's backbone, was not cut in the shape of a perfect rectangle. Its surfaces were slightly curved to make it thicker and deeper in the middle where the greatest weight would be placed. The tapering at the ends also gave it a more streamlined form which helped it to glide through the water. The sides of the keel were also notched to allow the lowest planks of the ship's 'skin' to fit snugly against it, as you can see in the diagram.

The planks that form the bottom and side 'skin' of a wooden ship are called strakes. The top diagram shows how strakes overlap each other. This is known as clinker, or clench, building and it is the method that appears always to have been used by the Vikings. (The other method of building a wooden ship, where the strakes lie edge to edge, and are held firm by being nailed to the ships' ribs, is called carvel building. Carvel planking could be thicker and was more suitable for heavy ships. It was the

method of shipbuilding used in the Mediterranean.) A clinker-built ship could have thin planking and still be water-tight. The strakes at the bottom of the Gokstad ship were only 2.6 cm (1 in.) thick, and slightly tapered at the edges where they overlapped each other. A groove was cut along the lower edge of each strake and this was packed with tarred wool before the planks were nailed together. This caulking was, of course, intended to make the planking water-tight. The nails or, more accurately, rivets were passed through both planks from the inside of the ship but, in the small spaces at bow and stern where a hammer could not be swung, the nailing had to be done from the outside. The strakes were not all the same. The tenth strake up from the keel had to be stronger because it was at the water-line, where the relatively flat under-water planking changed to the upright sides of the ship. This strake was 4.3 cm (1.7 in.) thick amidships. The fourteenth strake was also thicker because it contained the oarholes.

It looked as though the planking had been shaped and riveted together without being fixed to any framework. Only when the tenth strake was put in place, were the ribs put in position. They were not nailed to the strakes but tied with thin branches of willow. When the planks had been thinned, lumps (called cleats) had been left where the ribs were going to lie. Holes were drilled through these lumps, and the willow branches were fastened in these holes before being passed around the ribs. This method looked wobbly and surprised the discoverers of the ship. They doubted if it would be firm enough to endure Atlantic conditions and thought that the planks would rub together and become leaky.

What made the ship seem even less stout was the discovery that every other rib stopped at the tenth strake, so that above the water-line the planking was supported by only half the number of ribs that held the lower part in position.

Another feature that caused some doubt was the rudder, which was a large oar fixed to the side of the ship, near the stern. One can see how this rudder evolved by looking at rock carvings of more ancient ships. In the past, a man had stood in the stern and held an oar over the side of the vessel to steer it. This oar had gradually been made wider, but it took much strength to hold it in the right position in a rough sea. The Vikings overcame this problem by fastening its middle to the side of the ship. This fastening could not be rigid, as the rudder had to be twisted to change the direction of the ship; also the rudder could not stay down lower than the keel when the ship was being beached. A hole was drilled through the rudder, the ship's side and the reinforcing rib inside the ship. A thick, pliant willow branch was threaded through these holes and fastened at each end. This held the rudder close to the ship and yet allowed it to be turned. The willow fastening also acted as a pivot on which to swing the rudder into a horizontal position out of the water during beaching. But to prevent this from accidentally happening at sea and causing the steersman to lose control, a strap was passed around the top of the rudder and fastened at both ends to the gunwale. This knot could easily be untied during the beaching operation.

The holes for the ordinary oars were simple and yet clever. The crew obviously preferred to be able to push the oars, including the wide blades, through the holes from the inside, instead of having to pass them over the side and back into the ship. But large holes which would allow that were not wanted because the oars would bang around in them and they would let the waves gush through. The answer was to make small circular holes and to extend them with a diagonal cut through which the

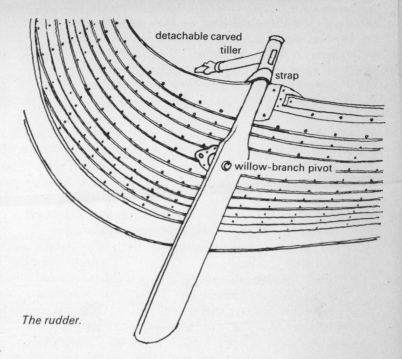

The rudder.

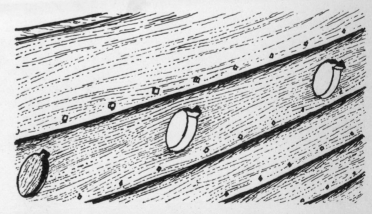

Oarholes, showing the extra pieces cut out to allow oar blades to be passed through from the inside.

oar blade could be pushed. Each hole had a small round shutter to block the water out when the ship was under sail.

The deck planking was not nailed down when the ship was excavated nor were there signs of nailholes. Loose planks were handy when stowing cargo beneath the deck. Although the ship was not able to carry any great bulk there was still enough room for quite a lot of relatively small objects. Every man could store his weapons under the deck at his rowing position. Here they would be dry and easily accessible. As there was no sign of any seating for the oarsmen, it has been suggested that each had his own sea chest containing his belongings to sit on. It has also been suggested that Vikings on other ships carried their belongings in tarpaulin kitbags. So, while the sea chest theory is fairly plausible, it is best to remember that there is no definite proof, nor do we know, for example, how the chests would have been secured to the deck.

There is a rack along the gunwale where the shields could be instantly available and where they could make a colourful display to deter would-be attackers. But when shields are placed on the Gokstad rack they cover the oarholes. It is therefore obvious that they were never displayed when the ship was being rowed. Also, if they were displayed while the ship was being sailed on the open sea, there was the danger that they might be torn away by a large wave. So, if the Gokstad ship ever did move with its shields on display, then it is most likely that this only happened in sheltered waters.

Though it told so much about how the Vikings built their ships, the Gokstad find gave no information about sails or rigging. Other finds since have proved no more helpful, so archaeologists have had to try to work out from other evidence how the sail was managed. It was a single square sail which must have been about ten metres long. Some people have guessed that Viking sails were made of linen, but most experts believe them to have been woollen because of the difficulty of producing flax in the north. Drawings and rock carvings usually show striped or diamond-patterned sails, and this is taken to represent reinforcing strips stitched to the sails, not merely decoration. The Vikings did like decoration, but strength was more important. A woollen sail would quickly stretch in some places and shrink in others. Leather, rope and linen have all been suggested as the reinforcing material, and perhaps all these materials may have been tried at one time or another. The sagas and other sources tell us that the sails were sometimes in two colours. So the reinforcing materials may have been dyed.

The method of reefing the sails is not known either. At sea, the wind often becomes too strong for full sails to be set, but having

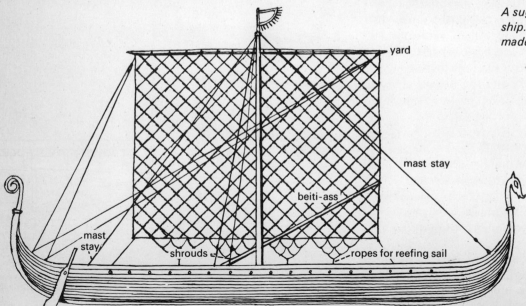

A suggested method of rigging a Viking ship. The diamond pattern on the sail is made by reinforcing strips.

yard

mast stay

beiti-ass

mast stay

shrouds

ropes for reefing sail

no sail at all does not produce much speed. The Vikings were such clever sailors that they must have had a method of using only a half sail or a quarter sail, and we can only assume that the methods they used were those used up to the end of the last century in north Norway. The fishermen used vessels that still looked like Viking ships. Their method of reefing sails was to use short ropes attached to the bottom edge of the sail. When the centre of these ropes was pulled, the two ends would come together, thereby bunching the sailcloth that was between. The rather indistinct picture stones of the Viking age (see page 51) show that they might have used a similar method of reefing.

We know from later finds that the mast on a Viking ship was held at the top by stays that ran to the prow and the gunwales. The Gokstad ship probably had stays, for the mast has been estimated to have been 12 metres (40 ft) high.

When the wind filled the big sail, there must have been considerable strain on the mast and stays and, through them, on the hull of the ship itself. It was particularly necessary to ensure that the mast was firmly held at its base. This meant that the shipbuilder had to take special precautions to prevent the hull from being damaged. The bottom of the mast rested on a heavy block of oak called the kerling (old woman). The kerling rested on the keel but was not fastened to it. It was fastened instead to two of the four ribs which also took some of its weight. As the whole block was 3.75 metres (12 ft 4 in.) long and 60 cm (2 ft) wide, the weight of the mast and sail was evenly distributed near the centre of the keel without pressing too hard at one particular point of it. There was a hole in the top of the kerling to hold the mast, and immediately forward of this hole the kerling was shaped into a raised platform. The raised piece helped to prevent the mast from leaning or sliding too far forward, but its main job was to provide a base for the mast fish.

The mast fish, so named because of its shape, was the largest single piece of wood in the structure. It was an oak block 5 metres (16 ft 6 in.) long and, in the middle, 1 metre (3 ft 3 in.) wide and ½ metre (20 in.) thick. The mast fish lay across four cross-beams which themselves have extra support from the kerling. It had an open slit in its top into which the mast could be slid. When the mast was in position, it was locked with a tight-fitting wedge.

After the Gokstad ship had been studied, it was possible to be certain about the design and workmanship of a Viking ship. The next step was to find out how it would behave at sea.

The mast fish of the Gokstad ship, with, below, a cross-section diagram to show how it worked.

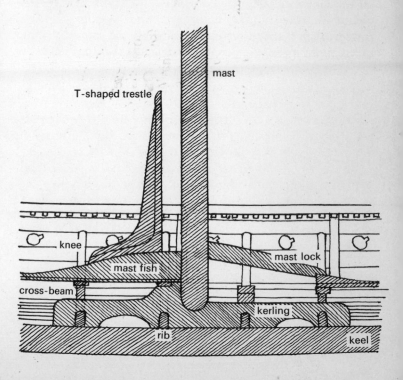

4 The voyage of *Viking*

'Viking' awaits her maiden voyage.

When the archaeologists had published all the facts about the Gokstad discovery, there was naturally much discussion among Norwegian historians and sailors about the efficiency of such a ship. Captain Magnus Andersen, a nautical writer with much experience of small boat sailing, conceived the idea of building a replica and sailing it across the Atlantic to visit the Chicago World Fair, planned to celebrate the four-hundredth anniversary of the 'discovery' of America by Columbus.

In the interests of comfort and safety, Andersen's replica differed in minor respects from the original, but he made no serious alterations to the design of the ship. The hull was strengthened by taking *all* the ribs up to the gunwale (page 11) and a spare rudder was provided that could be fixed to the stern, in case the steering oar proved unmanageable. There were also a few extra sails of modern design. Otherwise it would be an exact copy of the Gokstad ship that would sail the Atlantic.

The plan was that not only the design but also the materials should be accurately reproduced. They succeeded in building the ship of Norwegian oak except for the keel which came from America. The most difficult thing to get hold of was an oak wide enough for the mast fish. It was eventually found at Naes in Sandherred, not very far from Gokstad. Its dimensions give quite a good indication of what size materials the Vikings had been using. Three men spent a whole day getting it down. The trunk was 5 metres (16 ft 6 in.) long with a diameter of 1.5 metres (5 ft) at the root and more than 1 metre (3 ft 3 in.) at the top. Without branches it weighed four tonnes and the twigs and branches provided ten cartloads of materials.

The replica was launched in February 1893, and was called *Viking*. After a few weeks in Christiana (Oslo), taking on supplies and being visited by many sightseers, the ship was ready to be towed to Bergen, from where she would head for America.

Meanwhile the crew were appointed – Magnus Andersen in command, with two steersmen and nine other sailors. There were plenty of volunteers.

In one respect it was quite useful that *Viking* was in the water for so long before the main voyage started. Water leaked in at several places, and the reason for this was discovered. Some of the planks in the hull had bad knots. Since the building had taken place in severe frost and the materials had not been treated in advance, these had not been noticed. The leaks were fixed when the ship reached Bergen, and during the Atlantic crossing no more such trouble arose.

The real voyage started on Sunday 30 April. *Viking* was towed out of the Bergensfiord in company with thousands of small craft. At Marstein lighthouse the towrope was thrown and 'in a steady breeze from N.W. *Viking* was on its way due west at a speed of 6 knots'.

The voyage across the North Sea, 'with gentle changing winds', did not bring any incidents of importance. However, beyond the Shetlands the wind increased, and towards midnight it had reached gale force from the south-east. Sail had to be reduced, but before this was finished the ship had taken in a lot of water. The pump had to work all the time, and when it broke and was impossible to repair in the darkness, the crew had to use whatever scoops they had. The next morning the wind dropped. The ship had not been put to a very severe test but they had discovered that she was seaworthy. Their main uncertainty, the side rudder, had proved excellent.

With wind of changing strength and direction, sometimes in calm and sometimes in heavy seas, they proceeded westwards with no incidents of importance. Then, on the night between 8 and 9 May, *Viking* experienced her roughest weather of the whole voyage. We will use Magnus Andersen's own story:

'It blew up to a full storm, and the sea got rougher and rougher until about 4 o'clock it was in a turmoil. At this stage it was far from pleasant being on board. The sea washed over the boat again and again and we were soaked to the skin. A lot of this water found its way below and the pumps which we had managed to repair had to be watched carefully . . . In the afternoon we got periods of calmer weather and in the evening the storm decreased steadily in strength. The sail area was therefore increased and by 8 o'clock the following morning we were under full sail again. The wind had turned more westerly.'

The first few days of the third week at sea turned out to be the finest of the voyage. The wind was now from the east and the sea was calm. Apart from the normal sail, they set a top sail and others on both sides of the main sail to enable them to take full advantage of the good winds and thus be able to sail faster than the original Gokstad ship.

'The best progress of the whole voyage was made from 15 to 16 May when *Viking* sailed 223 nautical miles. This was fantastic sailing. During the night the northern lights were throwing their pale light over the sea whilst *Viking* was gliding like a seagull over the waves. We admired the movements of the ship and we noticed with pride the speed which sometimes reached eleven knots.'

The last week before Newfoundland was sighted they encountered changeable winds, often of gale force, and when they reached coastal waters there was no wind at all. For the last few days *Viking* had a S.S.W. breeze and entered into busy shipping 'lanes'. 'Here we got the opportunity to show how good a sailor she was and to our amazement she kept up with most of the other ships.'

After the voyage, Magnus Andersen wrote a book about his experience and one chapter was entitled, 'A few remarks about the ship, rudder and manoeuvrability'. The hull planking was not bolted to the ribs but tied on (page 11). This method of construction resulted in a very elastic hull which gave according to the movement of the ship. Very often in rough seas, the ship was twisted 15 cm (6 in.) to one side of its longitudinal axis but

the amazing thing was that no water leaked in. The twisting action could be seen along the deck-line and it was probably more noticeable on the original Gokstad ship which had some shorter ribs (page 14) and, as it seemed to writhe through the water, the ship may well have seemed like a serpent.

As far as sea worthiness and manoeuvrability are concerned, we can feel sure that *Viking* behaved as the Gokstad ship would have done. We cannot be so sure about the sails. Magnus Andersen reveals that during the days when the wind was blowing in the right direction, *Viking* was carrying every type of sail possible. When, in bad weather, they had to reduce sail it did not reduce the speed as much as they had expected. So they concluded that when the wind came from astern or from quarter astern there could not have been much difference between the sailing qualities of the copy and the original.

It was different, however, when the wind came from ahead. In such conditions a boat tends to turn up against the wind, and Magnus Andersen mentioned a few times that this was exactly what *Viking* tended to do. A modern jib sail makes it easier to counteract this and *Viking* was equipped with one. So Captain Andersen in this respect was unable to say certainly how the Gokstad ship would have behaved.

The voyage was a triumph. It had proved that the Vikings' ships could do what the sagas said they did. But many questions remained.

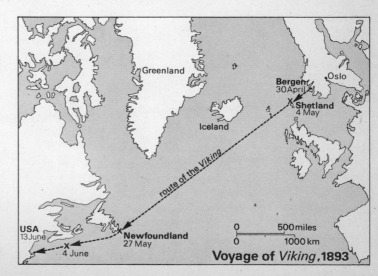

Voyage of *Viking*, 1893

5 The ancestors of the Gokstad ship

Now that everyone accepted that the Viking ship was a brilliantly designed vessel, the question arose as to how such an advanced design had been developed.

The discoveries of archaeologists help us to answer the question. Much of Scandinavia is poor land for crops and animals, but most of it is close to the sea, to fiords or lakes, so that with a boat it is easy to catch enough fish to supplement the diet. The Scandinavian people began building boats long before history began, and large fragments of some of them have been discovered. More information comes from drawings and carvings made on flat rocks.

◀ *Dug-out canoe, New Stone Age, from 3500 BC*
Many hollowed-out tree-trunk canoes have been found. But in some parts of Scandinavia there are few suitable trees.

Bronze Age, from 1500 BC ▶
Drawings from southern Norway seem to show boats made of animal skins, stretched over ribs of driftwood, rather like Eskimo umiaks. The bottom rib extended forward and upward to protect the skins when the vessel was beached. The boat was paddled by five kneeling men; the last man used his paddle to steer.

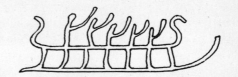

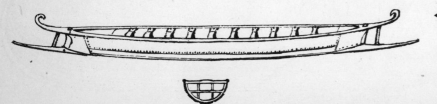

◀ *Hiortspring boat, about 350 BC*
This boat was found in a Danish bog. It was built of planks sewn together with cord, caulked with resin glue, and tied to ribs made from hazel branches. The bottom plank and gunwales projected at each end. There were twenty paddles, with steering paddles at each end.

Halsenoy boat, about AD 100 ▶

The fragments of a boat found at Halsenoy in Norway included wooden rowlocks; the change from paddling to rowing is very important. At about the same time rock carvings show the line of the projecting bottom plank (which helped to balance the boat and prevent damage from floating debris) curving upwards at the bow.

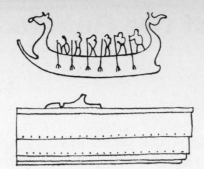

▲ Nydam ship, about AD 350

This ship was built up from a broad bottom plank. Its side planks overlap slightly, in clinker style, and are tied to strong, shaped ribs, while iron nails hold them together. The high prow and stern, and the steering oar, give the ship a Viking appearance. But it has no strong keel, so the hull was made very narrow to minimise pressure on it, and it would not have ridden the water easily. It would have been difficult to mount a mast on such a weak bottom.

Kvalsund ship, about AD 700 ▶

This ship had a true keel, strong enough to carry a mast. The hull was broader, and the steering oar firmly attached to a specially strengthened rib. The ship was nearly twenty metres (65 ft) long, its oak planks lashed or nailed to ribs of pine. Now the only further development needed was to shape the keel even more on the outside so that it would support a broader, flatter hull and a heavy mast.

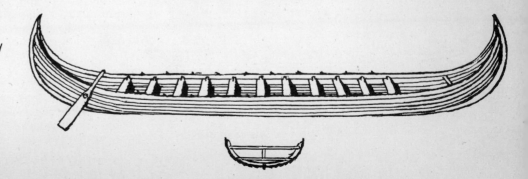

6 Different types of Viking ship

The Gokstad ship was so complete and her replica, *Viking*, had performed so well that it was easy for people to assume, without thinking, that all Viking ships were like this, that this was *the* typical Viking ship. But was it? Was it built to carry cargo, for instance? With sixteen oars on each side, what sort of crew would it need? Anyway, what type of ship would a great man want to be buried in—a fishing boat, a trading vessel, a warship? Was this the sort of ship that Eric the Red and his neighbours chose for their voyages? It was obvious, to anybody who stopped to think, that such good shipbuilders probably built varied types of ship for different purposes. Besides, the Viking period lasted for three or four hundred years. Ships had already developed during earlier centuries, and perhaps they were still developing. The only way to find out was by making more discoveries of ships.

The Oseberg ship

Another Viking burial ship, this one containing the skeleton of a woman, was found in 1904 at Oseberg, about 20 kilometres (12 miles) from Gokstad. The Oseberg ship is slightly smaller than the Gokstad ship, having fifteen pairs of oars. Although it was buried about the same time as the Gokstad find, it was an old ship when buried and was probably built about AD 800. It has been so well preserved that we know the oars, rudder and mast were new and unused when they were placed in the grave. It has been suggested that this was a little-used ship that had perhaps lain around in a boat-house for years before being specially re-equipped for the funeral.

The design of the Oseberg ship makes it less seaworthy than the Gokstad ship. Firstly, the keel is rather thin and, instead of being made in one piece, it is jointed. The stern-post is also made from two pieces. A further weakness of the hull is in the planking, which slants up from the keel and then turns sharply at the water-line, unlike the smooth curve of the Gokstad hull. The Oseberg oarholes are only about 10 cm (4 in.) from the water-line, and there is no sign that they ever had protective shutters. The kerling and other fittings for holding the mast are much smaller and weaker than in the Gokstad ship, and in

The tall, carved prow of the Oseberg ship, with a serpent's head at the centre of the spiral.

fact had at some time needed to be reinforced with iron bands. However, this would allow more space for people to move around on deck, if that was what the owner wanted. The oars are also short: the longest are 4 metres (13 ft 2 in.), compared with Gokstad's 5.85 metres (19 ft 2 in.). These oars were, however, decorated with a black painted pattern which would have been visible just outside the oarholes when in use. Another peculiarity of this ship is that the deck planks are all nailed down, except those nearest the mast, the stem and the stern. So, although it would have been easy for water to wash into the ship, it must have been awkward to get at the bilges to bale it out. Also, it would have been practically impossible to stow any stores or equipment below deck.

Taking all this evidence together, and feeling sure that the shipbuilders knew what they were doing, archaeologists have come to a fairly definite conclusion. They think that the ship was built for use in the sheltered waters of a fiord and perhaps for coasting in fine weather; that it was designed as a ship for pleasure or as a sign of the political greatness of its owner – a Viking royal yacht!

The Oseberg ship may be a poor example of Viking sea transport but it is the supreme example of Viking craftsmanship

A modern artist's impression of the Oseberg ship in coastal waters.

below: *A rib of the Oseberg ship. The ribs were fastened to cleats as in the Gokstad ship, but the weaknesses described opposite can be seen.*

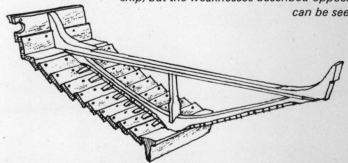

and ornamental design. The prow and stern sweep up 5 metres (16 ft 6 in.) above the water to a fine spiral. These high points would make the ship more difficult to steer in a cross-wind but they are famous for their wealth of carving on both sides. At the centre of the spiral on the prow is a serpent's head, the eyes painted to glow, and the stern spiral is in the form of a tail. Equipment buried with the ship included a ten kilo iron anchor, an oak gangplank and two large wooden water-casks. But, besides ship's equipment, there were all the worldly goods that a very rich woman would need in the next world, including the body of a servant. There were three studded oak chests with locks, three carved sleighs and a beautifully carved cart (see page 36). Horses, dogs and an ox had had their throats cut and been thrown on board.

The Ladby ship

The only Viking ship so far discovered buried in Denmark was at Ladby. Very little of its timber remained but the impression it had left in the soil showed the details of the hull remarkably well. Although it is only 2 metres (6 ft 6 in.) shorter than the Gokstad ship, it is only half as broad and it is much lighter. The distance between gunwale and keel is 0.65 metres (2 ft 2 in.) compared with 1.95 metres (6 ft 5 in.) on the Gokstad ship. Being so thin and shallow, it is obvious that this ship was not designed for cargo carrying nor for sailing rough seas but she could take the same number of rowers and, being lighter, she could be rowed faster. Without doubt she was a warship. Although she was apparently not as seaworthy as the Gokstad ship, Danes have

A replica based on the Ladby ship, built in Denmark by boy scouts in 1963.

built copies of the Ladby ship and sailed them across the North Sea. There is no evidence to suggest that there was any basic difference between Danish and Norwegian ships, and it must be remembered that the place where a ship was buried need not be the place where she was built.

The Skuldelev ships: the excavation

The most famous ship discovery in Denmark was not a burial. About the year 1000, the Peberrenden Channel of Roskilde Fiord was deliberately blocked, presumably as a defence measure. From that time a line of stones had extended across the channel near the village of Skuldelev and it had long been rumoured locally that there were wrecked ships there. A fragment of a ship had been found in the fiord in the 1920s but the first proper underwater investigation was not made until 1957. Frogmen reported finding four stone-laden wrecks and they were definitely dated as belonging to the end of the Viking period. As only part of the blockage had been investigated, it was hoped that further ships could be found. But the ships could not be successfully investigated or raised by frogmen because their nails were rusted away and much of the wood was soft. Also there were strong currents and poor underwater visibility.

It was therefore decided that the excavation area would have to be surrounded by a dam and then be drained. So, in 1959, the area was further investigated to find how large the dam would have to be. Stones were removed from the wrecks and mud was sucked away up pipes in a current of compressed air. Two more wrecks were found and the whole area mapped. Everything was then covered by stones and sand to protect it from water action and left until the final excavation could begin.

The dam was constructed in 1962 and it had a perimeter of 160 metres (175 yd). The water level was then lowered in stages and the topmost sand and stones were removed at each stage. If the water had all been drained immediately, the stones would have pressed more heavily on the wrecks and damaged them. Metal tools could not be used to remove the silt because much of the timber was too soft and the excavators used their hands. The wreckage was not moved immediately, as it had to be mapped and photographed. But, after nearly a thousand years under water, it would have crumbled on drying. Lawn sprinklers were installed all over the site and, for fifteen weeks, the excavators worked in a constant drizzle. Unfortunately for them, but luckily for the ships, the summer was the wettest and coldest for many years. Where possible, whole ships were uncovered and photographed before any timbers were removed but some timbers had to be moved to get at wreckage underneath. Wreck 2 had to be lifted to release part of wreck 1 beneath.

Wet timbers were placed in plastic tubes which were sealed at each end before being transported to a laboratory for preservation treatment. Although all nails had disappeared, some planks were still stuck together by mud or caulking and they were not separated. Other pieces, such as some keels, were too long and had to be cut before being transported. Everything was sprayed with a formalin solution to prevent rot before permanent treatment was undertaken at the laboratory.

If the ships were to be reassembled, it was important that during the preservation process, any timber shrinkage should be noticed so that nailhole could be matched with nailhole. There were thousands of pieces to be dealt with, and the action of ice and strong currents had broken and scattered many fragments of the ships about the floor of the channel. In fact, although the wrecks were numbered 1 to 6, it was discovered during excavation that 'wreck 4' was merely a large part of wreck 2 that had broken off and drifted some distance away. Each fragment was put on a large table at the laboratory and covered by a sheet of glass which in turn was covered with a sheet of transparent polythene. The outline of the piece and any significant marks were traced on the polythene. This work went on for five years and over two kilometres of polythene were used.

Some timber needed special treatment even before its polythene pattern was drawn. The keels were warped and twisted into undulating shapes because the fiord bottom was uneven and the ships had been pressed hard against it. The first keel was put in a warm tank where the preservative was softened but the wood itself was held in a press. The bulges were corrected and the preservative reapplied. But, when the other timbers were placed against the keel, they did not fit. So the whole process had to be done again. The whole reassembly could be likened to a large jigsaw puzzle in which every piece had been distorted and partially destroyed.

Most shipwrecks have remains of cargo and ships' fittings strewn about the sea bed, but these ships had been deliberately sunk and therefore stripped beforehand; even the deck planking had been removed. Initially, three ships had been sunk and

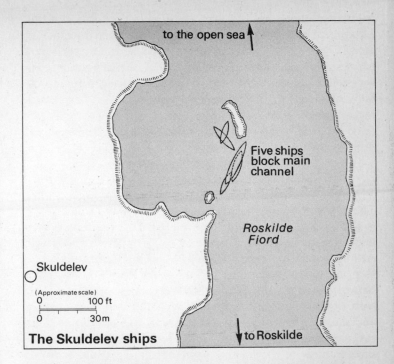

to the open sea

Five ships block main channel

Roskilde Fiord

Skuldelev

(Approximate scale)
0   100 ft
0   30m

The Skuldelev ships

to Roskilde

Excavations of the Skuldelev ships in progress within the coffer dam.

pointed stakes had been driven into the fiord bed beside them and through them, so that currents could not move them. Some of the stones were probably on board as they sank, but many more were added to the wreckage. It is believed that the upper parts of the ships were visible above the surface and they were damaged by ice. Two more ships were added later to improve the blockage, and one of these lay over the ice-worn timbers of a lower ship. The blockage had been designed expertly, and matched other blockages in Roskilde Fiord as part of a large defensive plan. It remained effective until 1962.

Although the ships were difficult and expensive to recover and in a poor state of preservation, they have yielded much extra information. Each ship is different. There are two warships, one being the longest Viking ship yet discovered; a small ship that was probably either a ferry or a fishing boat; and two cargo vessels.

The Skuldelev ships: the merchantmen

Wreck 1 is probably the most important of the Skuldelev ships. It is a knorr, or heavy cargo ship. We knew, from the Icelandic sagas, that such ships had existed and that the size of their cargoes could not have been greatly exaggerated because the settlers crossing the Atlantic could not have survived with much less equipment and livestock. Wreck 1 is the only example we have of a Viking ship that could have carried such a cargo.

We will never know if this ship ever did cross the Atlantic to Iceland, but it is highly probable. All other Viking ships have many marks of scraping on their bottoms, which suggest that they were frequently beached, but this one shows very few. She would be very heavy to drag up a beach, and she was a deep sea ship. Therefore it is assumed that she was used more in the North Sea and Atlantic than the Baltic.

The maximum length of the ship was 16.5 metres (54 ft), width 4.8 metres (15 ft 9 in.) and height from keel to gunwale 1.9 metres (6 ft 3 in.). The maximum draught when fully loaded would have been about 1.5 metres (5 ft). She had decks fore and aft with an open hold amidships 5.5 metres (18 ft) long. This would allow a cargo of up to 35 cubic metres (1,200 cu. ft) to be carried and there was also some space beneath the decks. However, some of this space would be needed for sleeping quarters on a long voyage.

The knorr had to depend almost entirely on her single square

Skuldelev wreck 1 revealed on the fiord bottom, and, below, as reconstructed in the museum.

sail, and we have already seen that Captain Magnus Andersen in *Viking* had needed more than this. However, it is known from the sagas that the Vikings had something called a *beiti-ass*, apparently a spar which held one corner or edge of the sail forward, so that the ship could sail closer to the wind. (Sailors have used the expression 'beating to windward' ever since the Vikings used the beiti-ass.) It is not definitely known how it was used, and the remains of a beiti-ass have never been identified. However, nailed to the inside of the port side of wreck 1, forward and just above the deck was a piece of timber 1.25 metres (4 ft 1 in.) long with three notches. Probably, this was to take the beiti-ass at three settings.

The kerling of this ship is not now preserved as it was removed from the wreckage in 1924 by fishermen who were trying to clear the channel. It was recognised and photographed then, but was destroyed in the Second World War. It was estimated to have originally been just over 5 metres (16 ft 6 in.) long, and to have extended over six ribs. There was no trace of a mast fish, so it is presumed that the mast was held by an arrangement of crossed beams. This would have had the advantage of allowing more cargo space, and it would be quite practical on a ship which did not have its mast raised or lowered often.

There were also a few oarholes on this ship both fore and aft. Some of the planking was missing here, but it is estimated that there would be at least two pairs of oars both fore and aft. Of course there were no traces of oarholes in the cargo section amidships. The ship was very heavy and the oars would not be used very much.

The planks are pine and, since pine is rare in Denmark and plentiful in Norway, it is presumed that the ship was built in Norway. Oak was used for the keel, kerling, stem and ribs. The ribs were nailed to the planks and not tied as in the case of the Gokstad ship. This difference appeared on all the Skuldelev ships and it may be that this method of building (not entirely unknown at an earlier date) was now preferred by Viking shipbuilders. It is thought that this knorr was built not before 950, and possibly several decades later.

The other cargo vessel, wreck 3, though smaller, is better preserved, and radio-carbon dating shows that she was built some years later than the knorr. She was built entirely of oak. The total length was 13.5 metres (44 ft), and she was 3.2 metres (10 ft 6 in.) broad with a maximum draught of 1 metre (3 ft 3 in.).

One interesting feature of this ship is that extra timbers had

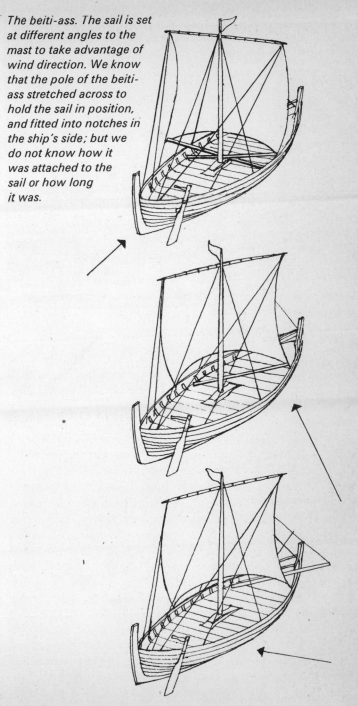

The beiti-ass. The sail is set at different angles to the mast to take advantage of wind direction. We know that the pole of the beiti-ass stretched across to hold the sail in position, and fitted into notches in the ship's side; but we do not know how it was attached to the sail or how long it was.

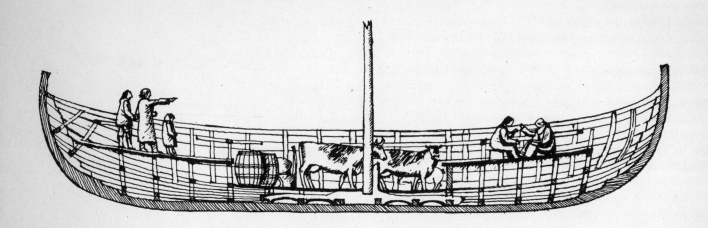

A knorr, based on the Skuldelev wreck 1, shown in section. The heavy cargo is carried amidships, and a tarpaulin covering would be rigged to keep out some of the water.

been used to strengthen places where there would be most strain. Where the bottom of the ship curved up to the sides, a specially thick strake had been provided in the Gokstad ship, for instance (page 10). In wreck 3 reinforcing pieces were nailed at this point instead, which was probably easier and saved weight. There were also extra cross-beams and a partition on each side of the open cargo area amidships, and a specially strong cross-beam to support the mast.

This ship also shows how the shrouds which ran from the mast top were fixed to the ship's sides. There were two cleats nailed to the outside of the gunwales. A complete wooden ring made out of willow was found passing through a hole in the middle of a cleat and then through a hole in the gunwale and back to the cleat. To prevent rubbing, the shroud would have been attached to the ring and not to the side. The fact that these cleats are outside the gunwales suggests that this ship did not often tie up where the cleats could have been damaged by bumping against a jetty. Also the bottom of the hull was much scraped, which indicates that it was beached many times.

There are only seven oarholes on this ship: two forward on the starboard, three forward on the port and one each side aft. Only the pair just forward of the cargo space showed signs of wear; presumably these were the most convenient positions from which to manoeuvre the ship, for example when turning in a narrow creek. The oarholes are square; not the best shape for rowing, but convenient on this ship; the oar blades could be passed through diagonally and yet the hole was small enough to prevent undue banging.

The Skuldelev ships: the warships

Wreck 5 was built as a warship. It was about 18 metres (60 ft) long but only 2.6 metres (8 ft 6 in.) broad. The ratio of length to breadth is that of a warship, not a merchant ship. Besides, this ship had a complete deck and rack for shields.

The keel was unusual. It was made in three pieces. The main piece was 11.9 metres (39 ft) long and was joined to a slightly curved forward piece, 2.7 metres (8 ft 10 in.) long, and a similarly curved piece aft which was 0.8 metre (2 ft 8 in.) long. The forward piece is less worn so it was probably a replacement after damage. There were also many repairs to the old planking. Short pieces were inserted in long planks and patches were placed over scrapes and holes. Old nailholes were still visible in reused planks and the gunwale had a line of round oarholes blocked permanently with oak plugs. These holes could never have been used on this ship because the cross-beams would have impeded the rowers, while the real oarholes are so placed that the rowers could have used the cross-beams as seats. There were probably twelve oars on each side. Little can be discovered about the mast arrangements.

Wreck 2 is a similar vessel but it had been about 28 metres (92 ft) long and is therefore the longest Viking ship ever found. Unfortunately it was in a bad state of preservation. Perhaps some timbers and planking had been removed to be reused on other ships before the wreck was sunk. The remains consist of one endpiece, presumed to be the stern, parts of the keel, kerling and lower strakes, and some ribs and their knees.

The kerling was no less than 13.3 metres (43 ft 8 in.) long. It appears to have been made deliberately long to reinforce the hull longitudinally. This could have been done by using a thicker keel but that would have made the ship heavier. Every effort was made to save weight. Even the knee pieces were cut so as to get rid of any wood that did not seem necessary.

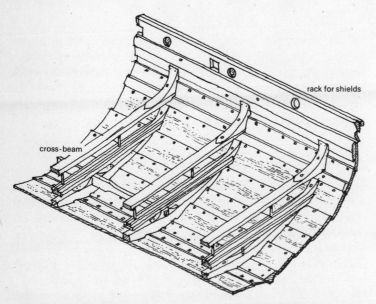

Planking of the Skuldelev warship showing the strakes, which were thin to save weight, the blocked oar-holes and the cross-beams.

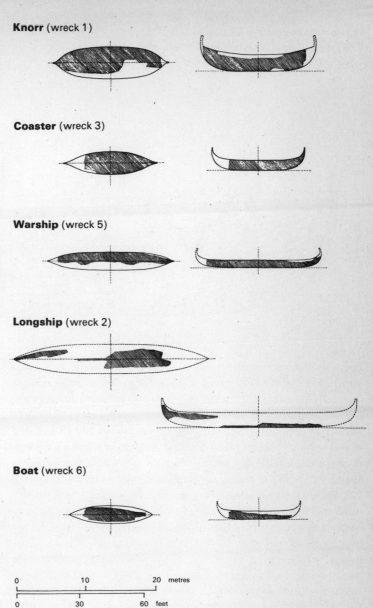

Knorr (wreck 1)

Coaster (wreck 3)

Warship (wreck 5)

Longship (wreck 2)

Boat (wreck 6)

rack for shields

cross-beam

| 0 | 10 | 20 | metres |
| 0 | 30 | 60 | feet |

These drawings of the Skuldelev ships show the parts recovered and the suggested original shapes. Compare the long, thin fighting ships with the short, squat cargo vessels.

25

It is estimated that the ship was about 4.5 metres (15 ft) wide and carried 50 to 60 men. Because none of the upper parts remain, we have no proof that the ship could be rowed but it is safe to assume that any ship of these dimensions was a warship, or a longship as they are called in the sagas, and these invariably had oars. This long, lightly built galley, much more specialised than the Gokstad ship, gives us an idea of the ships that fought in the great sea battles of the later part of the Viking period, which will be described later.

Small craft

The last ship of the Skuldelev wreckage, wreck 6, was built of pine with an oak keel. Being softwood, it had splintered badly and the fragments that have been pieced together have been insufficient to allow us to feel sure of its purpose. The bow and stern are missing but there are no oarholes in the midship section where they would be needed if it was a warship. It had a rounded bottom giving it a shallow draught and a very small kerling, about 1.32 metres (4 ft 4 in.) long, presumably for a small mast.

It is thought that it was used for short distances, and it may have been a fishing boat or a ferry. Whatever it was used for, its capacity had been increased after it was built because the sixth strake was originally the gunwale strake but a seventh strake had been added.

The fact that we cannot positively identify this ship reminds us of the many differing uses the Vikings had for ships and boats. They would have learnt to use rowing boats at a very early age and continued to use them throughout their lives. The presence of three of them in the Gokstad burial shows they were still considered to be useful after death. All three of these were made of oak but are of different lengths: 6.5, 8 and 9.75 metres (21 ft 4 in., 26 ft 3 in. and 29 ft 7 in.). The largest was rowed by three pairs of oars and the smallest by two. They were fitted with side rudders like the ship. All three were lightly built, the planking of the largest boat being between only 8 and 15 millimetres (about ½ in.) thick. The variety of design and the careful workmanship revealed in all these ships and boats show us that Viking shipbuilders must have been men of great experience, intelligence and skill.

26

7 Building a Viking ship

The master of a shipyard was called a shipwright. He would be in charge of a group of workers who built larger ships. A smaller boat would be built by a single man just as wooden boats are made today in fiord-side boat sheds. The largest ships were built on stocks which were left in place after the ship was finished, presumably for another ship to be built on them. The stocks which were used for the famous *Long Serpent* were still in position at Trondheim 200 years later. She was built in AD 1000, was 37 metres long and carried 200 men.

The shipwright who built *Long Serpent* was called Thorberg Skafhogg, but the sagas state that there were many others to help him. 'Some to fell wood, some to shape it, some to make nails, some to carry timber.' The most skilled workers would work on the keel, stem and stern. The *filungar*, who made the planking, received smaller wages than the skilled workers, but the timber carriers probably got the least.

The shipwright would be constantly on the look-out for suitable timber. A keel would come from a straight-growing tree, but timber with a natural bend in the grain was valuable for making ribs. Growing trees would be remembered for future cutting while trees that had reached the right size would be cut down and their timber stored in water until it was needed. Timber stores in lakes and bogs have been discovered in a number of places. Sometimes the timber has been partly worked and, in some places, completed ships' stems have been found, like the one from the Isle of Eigg in the Hebrides (page 29).

A good ship would be made completely of oak, but so many ships were made that oak became scarce and pine, ash, birch, alder, lime and willow were used for various parts in many ships. The keel, however, was invariably of oak because it was not only the backbone of the ship but also the part that was most scraped as the ship was dragged ashore. The other parts that took a lot of strain were the stem and stern, the kerling and the frames. So oak was preferred for these parts.

The shortage of oak trees in Norway today seems to be the

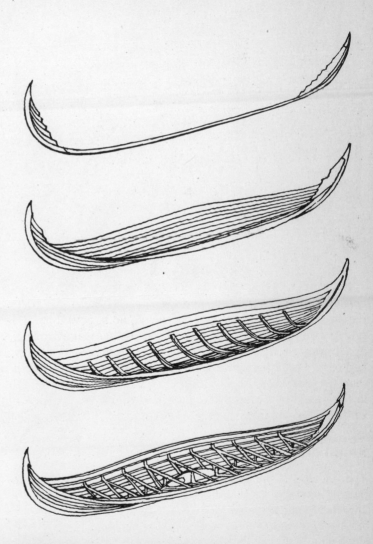

Building stages of the Skuldelev coaster. We know that the strakes were fitted before the ribs because they were nailed together from the inside, and many of the nails were subsequently covered by ribs.

Stempiece found in a bog on the Isle of Eigg, Hebrides. This was unused, and appears to have been shaped and then stored in the water. It is 202 cm (6 ft 8 in) long.

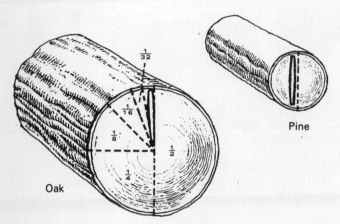

Wood-splitting techniques, as revealed by a study of the grain of Skuldelev planks.

result of so many trees having been felled in the past thousand years to make ships. One can imagine Thorberg Skafhogg having all sorts of difficulties in finding a tree to provide the keel for the largest ship ever seen in Norway in the year AD 1000. If he had to have joints in the keel, then he would want them as far from the mast as possible. It is interesting to note that, although longships were built after *Long Serpent*, none quite reached her record length.

Thorberg's timber carriers would not have been merely shipyard labourers, but men who travelled long distances into the forests to cut down the trees that had been earmarked by Thorberg and his friends. Winter was probably the best time to bring the timber out of the forests because it could be slid along the snow and there would be less undergrowth to hamper movement. When the trees were cut down, the branches would have to be trimmed off before transportation could begin. But, sometimes, the trunks themselves would be split along their length to ease the task of carrying. It makes sense to chip off all the wood that is not needed. Although the planks may have been made in the forest, the shipwright would want to supervise the cutting of the important shapes such as the keel. The timber carriers would therefore sometimes bring in whole trunks and sometimes partly finished planks.

Close examination of the wood of the Viking ships that have been found so far has revealed no trace of saw marks. It has been concluded that the shipbuilders used only axes, gouges, adzes, planes, draw knives and augers. Examination of oak planks has shown that the trees were split along their length into halves, then quarters, then eighths and so on until a wide trunk gave thirty-two planks. Pine trees, however, were split once only, and each semi-circular piece shaved down into one plank.

Once there was a stock of wood at the waterside, then the keel could be laid down. The shape of the keels changed during the Viking times. The Gokstad keel is rectangular in section, with grooves in the sides to allow the bottom strake on each side to fit into it. A hundred years later, we find the keel with a T-shaped cross-section amidships, perhaps to absorb better the weight of the kerling. The weight, strength and handling qualities of the ship would be seriously affected by a badly shaped keel. The shipwright would be closely involved with the keel laying. He would also closely supervise the fitting of the stem and stern, as these parts took a buffeting on the ocean and on beaching.

The next job was making the sides of planking. This outer

skin of planks was fitted before the interior ribs were put in position. It is probable that wooden shapes called templates were held against the planks when they were bent into position to ensure that the correct symmetry of the ship was maintained. The planking of the Gokstad ship shows that each plank was specially cut to fit into an exact place in the ship. When the planking was finished the ribs could either be tied in position with spruce roots or nailed in (often with wooden pegs or tree-nails).

This part of the job, although it called for careful craftsmanship by the workers, did not need such close supervision; a badly made plank could always be noticed and replaced. Nevertheless, the different shapes and thicknesses of the strakes in different parts of the ship needed a skilled eye. We know from the sagas that Thorberg had to go home and stayed there a long time while *Long Serpent* was being planked. When he returned, he went in the evening with King Olaf to look at the ship.

'Everybody said that never was seen so large and so beautiful a ship of war. . . . Early next morning the king returned again to the ship, and Thorberg with him. The

carpenters were there before them, but all were standing idle with their arms across. The king asked what the matter was. They said that the ship was all spoilt; for somebody had gone from stem to stern, and cut one deep notch after the other down the one side of the planking. When the king came nearer he saw that it was so, and said, with an oath, that the man should die if the king learnt who had spoilt the vessel from sheer malice – "and I shall bestow a great reward on whoever can tell me about this" . . .

Thorberg says, "I will tell you, king, who did it. I did it myself."

The king says, "Thou must restore it all to the same condition as before, or thy life shall pay for it."

Then Thorberg went and chipped the planks until the deep notches were all smoothed and made even with the rest; and the king and all present declared that the ship was much handsomer on the side of the hull which Thorberg had chipped, and bade him to shape the other side the same way.'

Obviously, the less experienced filungar had made the planks

HIC TRAHVNT:NAVES.ADMA RE

Three stages in shipbuilding, as depicted in the Bayeux Tapestry: cutting and shaping timbers, fixing and trimming planks with adze, axes and drill, and launching. The tapestry is 50 cm (nearly 20 in.) deep.

too thick for Thorberg's satisfaction. By shaving them down, he had made the ship lighter to row and faster to sail.

The kerling had next to be fitted in the bottom of the ship. As we have seen, not only had it got a shallow socket to hold the mast bottom but it also had a vertical support to hold the mast upright. The wood for the kerling had to be specially chosen with this support growing from it. In all the ships so far discovered the kerling has been a natural growth. An arm made from a separate piece of wood would be weaker, and in this part of the ship a break could have disastrous effects. Finding a suitable piece of wood for a ship the size of *Long Serpent* must have given Thorberg and his men a difficult search.

While the kerling took the full weight of the mast, either a mast fish or strong cross-beams had to be fitted at deck level to help to hold it steady. It seems much more likely that *Long Serpent* would have had cross-beams, like the Skuldelev ships.

With the arrangements for holding the mast safely in hand, work could continue on finishing the upper part of the ship. Besides oarholes and shield rack, holes or cleats had to be provided on the gunwale for the ropes holding the mast and sail. Inside the ship, deck planking could be put down: it would have

to be cut very carefully, to reduce the amount of water that could trickle through when waves broke across the deck, and this would be especially important where the planks were not nailed down. One of the final jobs before launching would be the fitting of the rudder, which had to be the right size to control the ship, and well balanced so that the steersman could handle it easily.

Launching the ship would be an easy task to men who were used to dragging ships overland and who often beached and refloated ships.

Two important jobs have not been mentioned because they would be going on all the time the ship was being built. These were nail-making and tarring. The timber may have been freshly cut or, more probably, it had been kept in water. Either way, it would dry out and perhaps warp if not properly treated. Tarring was therefore a regular task for both shipbuilder and sailor. In forest areas, the tar could be made from pine resin but, in the tree-less areas of the north Atlantic, seal oil may have been used as a substitute at times.

Both iron and wood were used for nails. There was a tendency to use small iron nails to join lighter, thinner parts such as planks, but heavier parts like cross-beams and kerlings were held with wooden pegs, or tree-nails. Wood was preferred for heavy jobs, where a lot of strain came on one fastening, because it would not rust and its expansion and contraction would not differ from that of the blocks in which it was placed. Most important, it would be less brittle and less likely to snap than iron.

The sails and ropes would have been made while the ship was being built on the stocks. Both whale skin and seal skin are known to have been used for ropes, with wooden rings at their fastenings. As no remains of sails have yet been discovered, we cannot be certain as to how they were made. Spinning and weaving of clothing textiles was women's work, but sail repairs on a voyage would have to be done by men, so perhaps the spinning of ropes and weaving of sails was undertaken by both sexes. Certainly, shipbuilding involved a thousand and one jobs, and any help available would be used.

The ship would have to be furnished with such things as a gangplank, water-barrel and oars. In a warship, the oars would have to be of different lengths, those towards stem and stern longer than the midship ones so that the blades could enter the water in a straight line and not in a curve like the bulging sides of the ship. Calculating the exact length of oars for each pair of oarholes would create a problem. Perhaps the oars were made slightly longer than necessary and shortened after being tried in the ship.

Other equipment would depend on the owner's wishes. A ship like *Long Serpent* would probably be decorated so as to look especially impressive. But most Viking ships were, we think, quite plain—we should not be deceived by the Oseberg ship, which was probably very unusual. More serviceable 'extras' would be needed according to the task. Ships going on long voyages, for example, would require tarpaulins to cover their cargoes and, perhaps, tents. These could sometimes have been old or spare sails,or they might be taken from another ship.

Once the owner had received his ship, it would be his job to look after it and especially to inspect it before laying it up for the winter. Iron rusts, wooden pegs can become worn with friction, and nailholes must have enlarged as the nails rubbed and moved in them. Planks would be scraped or splintered, or parts might rot. Loose nails would have to be pulled out and replaced by larger ones. When the problem was really bad, worn planks would have to be replaced. Many of the excavated ships,

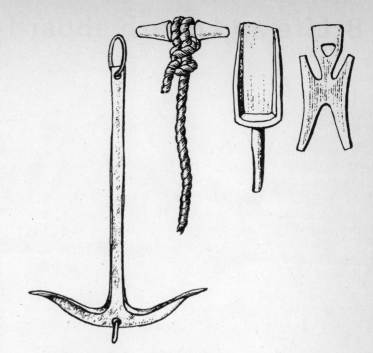

Anchor (102 cm (40 in.) long), rope cleat, baler and rope block from the Gokstad and Oseberg ships.

as we saw, had been repaired. Sometimes damage was not only caused by natural wear and tear. The Skuldelev knorr had one interesting hole, driven through the planking from the outside and into the framework, which had been repaired with a bung; from its shape and size, it is believed that the hole had been caused by an arrow. As part of the regular overhaul the bottom would be scraped and cleaned before the ship was retarred. All the equipment, too, would have to be checked. Winter indoor jobs would have been making new ropes for when they were needed, and repairing sails.

The shipwright would be unlikely to have anything to do with the vessel after its first launching. Repairs would normally be done by the owner and his men. But it is possible that the shipwright would be called to do a large repair. There is a story of a twelfth-century Norwegian king who got a shipwright to cut a ship in two and insert a new midship to make the vessel longer – a technique called 'ship surgery' in modern shipyards.

8 Life and death aboard ship

We saw in the opening chapters how the Vikings used their ships to navigate the north Atlantic and discover Greenland and America. Later we saw that, although the Gokstad type of ship was capable of crossing the Atlantic, it is more likely that Eric the Red and his people used ships like the Skuldelev knorr. But this was only one small part of Viking sea-borne enterprise.

It is impossible to give a general picture of what life was like aboard a Viking ship because, not only were the ships of different types and sizes, but they sailed into different geographic areas. The fur trader in the White Sea could be having trouble with pack ice, while other Vikings, after sailing down great rivers, were loading polar furs onto camels by the Caspian Sea for the journey across the desert to the market at Baghdad.

Ships differed from one another because different men set sail for different reasons. The owner of the Gokstad ship could have used his ship on one trip as a trader bringing furs or silver to market at Hedeby in Denmark. His next trip to sea could be as a pirate and he could even change his mind in the middle of a voyage if the opportunity for greater profit arose. So the trader could become pirate and the pirate could become trader. That would be easy with a ship like the Gokstad. Others, as we have seen, were too specialised. Few Vikings would choose to use a longship for trading or a knorr for fighting.

Atlantic seafaring

Let us try first to imagine life aboard a merchant knorr in the Atlantic. The size and condition of the cargo could affect living conditions. The more cargo, the less space for sleeping. A small ship carrying animals, particularly goats, could be very unpleasant, especially in warm weather.

Perhaps the very worst type of voyage was with an emigrating family across the Atlantic with all their belongings, food and water, their cattle and sheep, animal food and perhaps even some timber for building their houses. Passengers and animals could be sharing part of the cargo space beneath the tarpaulins in the middle of the ship. There could be as many as twenty passengers, half a dozen small cows and a small flock of sheep and goats soaking and shivering together. It is true that a knorr had two small triangular spaces like kennels beneath the fore deck and after deck. These spaces would be about 1 metre (3 ft) high and 4 metres (13 ft) wide as one entered them. They would be about 4 metres (13 ft) long as well but, as one went further in, they became narrower and lower. These spaces could be very wet, especially on older ships and they would be dark. Nevertheless, passengers probably preferred sleeping in them to being beneath the tarpaulins with the animals – if the crew left any space for them.

The size of the crew would vary according to the size of the ship and the dangers of the voyage. Besides handling sails or oars, or weapons when necessary, men would be needed on some voyages for almost constant baling. Most of the water would collect in the central section where the animals were and many Viking sailors must have spent much of their time at this boring, unpleasant task, working often beneath tarpaulins made of hides. And, to add to their discomforts, there were apparently no means of cooking on these ships.

One would expect that, having reached the coasts of their destinations, the settlers would be very quick to disembark from such ships, but this was not always so. Ingolf Biornolfsson, the first settler to arrive in Iceland, is said to have thrown his seat posts overboard with a prayer to the god Thor. He did not land his belongings until the posts were found on the beach and then he started to build his home at that beach. He was following the rules of his religion and he was also being a very practical sailor. His seat posts showed him where the on-shore currents were to be found. These currents would bring in driftwood and, more importantly, would help to beach a fishing boat in stormy weather. Ingolf's wisdom is shown by the fact that with all the

coastline to choose from, he chose the spot that was to become Iceland's capital city, Reykjavik.

Of course, Ingolf was lucky. His voyage was successful. Some voyages ended in disaster. It is impossible now to estimate the percentage of unsuccessful voyages, but it was probably fairly low. We know of Icelanders who made the return trip to Norway on numerous occasions and who survived to die in their beds. Nevertheless, the dangers were great. We know of two occasions when Eric the Red was in serious trouble – when he lost half his fleet when leading the colonists to Greenland and when he sailed in a circle in the north Atlantic (pages 4 and 7). But it was his son, Leif, who was called 'the Lucky'. According to the saga, he saw something strange in the distance when he was returning from his first voyage of discovery to Vinland. When he altered course and came closer, he discovered a ship's crew standing on a reef. They must have been blown many hundreds of miles off course and wrecked, and were saved by the very first Viking ship deliberately to set course for that part of the ocean. Their chances of being rescued must have been one in many million but it was Leif and not Thorir, the wrecked captain, who was given the nickname of 'Lucky'. This was probably because Thorir and most of his crew were not able to survive the following winter in Greenland.

Another tale of slow death by shipwreck comes from the saga of Thorfinn Karlsefni which states:

'Because of the tempest, Biarni Grimolfsson drifted with his ship to the Irish Sea, and they met a breaker, and the ship began to go down. They had a small boat greased with tar which protects against sea worms. They entered the boat but realised that it could not carry all of them. Then said Biarni, "whereas the boat cannot carry more than half our men, it is my advice that lots should be cast to settle who should go into the boat, because this cannot be settled by rank." They all thought this very fair, so nobody objected. So they drew lots and it fell to Biarni's share to go in the boat with half the men.'

Accidents could even happen in sheltered fiords and the Ynglinga saga tells of one:

'King Eystcin was sitting at the helm as they sailed past Jarlsö, and another ship was sailing at the side of his, when there came the stroke of a wave, by which the beiti-ass of the other ship struck the king and threw him overboard, which proved his death. His men fished up his body, and it was carried into Borre, where a mound was thrown up over it.'

The life of a Viking seafarer, even in moments of apparent security and even on peaceful voyages, could be very uncomfortable and dangerous. Probably life was hardest of all aboard the ships that dared to cross the grey wastes of the north Atlantic.

Real Viking crews

Though we nowadays use the word loosely to describe all the Scandinavians for a period of several centuries, 'Viking' really refers to those seafarers who went adventuring to seek wealth by whatever method seemed most appropriate – including theft, trickery and murder. A real Viking had to be prepared for violence, and often forced others to behave as he did.

Vikings were in the habit of undertaking coastal voyages without provisions. When they were hungry, they would go ashore and steal the nearest animals on the beach and cook them. They called this 'strand-hogg' which means beach-kill. The owners of the animals often could not move their stock to safety because the only grazing available was beneath the cliffs at the fiord-side. So they could only be well prepared to fight off the robbers and to sail after them as they fled, to dissuade them from ever choosing those particular fields again. This sort of work demanded ships like the Gokstad or the Ladby.

As farmsteads became better armed, so ships became better armed, and the temptation to attack and rob other ships grew. So ships became larger in order to carry more fighting men. Naturally this had its consequences for the rulers of the land: if any jarl (earl) wanted to be master in his district, he would need the biggest ship in the district, and so the king would need even larger ships if he was to rule over the jarls.

Despite the cost of feeding warriors through the winter, a rich Viking had to maintain them or else be at the mercy of his neighbours. Erling Skialgsson was the brother-in-law of King Olaf Tryggvason who ruled in Norway from 995 to 1000. According to the sagas:

'Erling always had with him 90 freeborn men or more; and both winter and summer it was the custom in his house to drink at the midday meal according to a measure, but at night there was no measure in the drinking. When the earl was in the neighbourhood he had 300 men or more. He never went to sea with less than a fully manned ship of 20 benches of rowers. Erling also had a ship of 32 benches of rowers, which was besides very large for that size, and which he used on Viking cruises, or on an expedition; and in it were 200 men at the very least.'

It seems that a Viking crew was always made up of freeborn men because it would be too easy for slaves to rebel on a ship or to desert during a battle. The free man, however, lived very comfortably with his leader and he knew that when his leader was attacked, it was his duty to defend him. This was how he paid for his comfortable, idle existence. Cowardice could mean death or, worse still, expulsion as a nithing (contemptible person). On the other hand, the bravest warriors sat nearest their leader in the hall and this was a favoured position, especially in winter when their leader was nearest the fire. If a man was to be punished, the company could decide that he was to be moved farther down the table. The man at the bottom of the table was often the object of much scorn and could be pelted with meat bones. (The Archbishop of Canterbury was pelted with bones by Vikings in 1013.)

Although they would eat their leader's meat and fight for him to the death, Vikings were very proud of their freeborn status and would not bow to any man. It is said that a stranger went to a crew under a flag of truce and asked for their leader; he received the reply that they were all leaders. There is also a story, that may or may not be true, about Rollo taking Normandy in 911. When the terms of peace had been agreed between Rollo and the French king, the new duke was supposed to kneel and kiss the king's foot as an act of fealty. Rollo could not do this as it would mean that he would lose the respect of his men. So he got his steward to do it for him. But the steward, being a free man, had his own ideas, so he grabbed the king's foot and pulled it up to his mouth, while the king fell backwards off his seat.

The main entertainment of Viking crews was drinking and they also loved a good joke, especially if it was rough and a trick against someone else. Their life could be grim at times but they made merry in their own fashion. They liked wrestling, which is

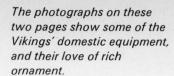

The photographs on these two pages show some of the Vikings' domestic equipment, and their love of rich ornament.

left: The magnificently carved sledge and cart from the Oseberg ship burial. The sledge is 2 m (6 ft 7 in.) long by 74 cm (2 ft 5 in.) high; the cart, 2.9 m (9 ft 6 in.) long by 1.35 m (4 ft 5 in.) high.

right: An amulet shaped like Thor's hammer.

below: A necklace of silver filigree beads from Gotland.

still done according to their rules in Iceland and in Cumbria in England. A game which they enjoyed on board ship when the oars were put out was running along the oars. The runner always raised a laugh when he slipped and fell into the water. There were also quieter entertainments; a gaming board was found on the Gokstad ship.

When they were at home, crews who followed important jarls ate their way through a lot of farm produce which their leaders collected as taxes for protecting the countryside. But the farmers were themselves the same breed as the Vikings, and would refuse if the demands were too great. About 970, Erling, the brother of

King Harald Greycloak of Norway, tried to use force to collect his tax. But the farmers retaliated, attacked the Vikings while they were feasting, and killed Erling and many of his men.

It was unusual for a Viking crew to lose their lives like that, at home, but not so unusual to lose them when they went raiding. Saint Olaf's saga tells a typical story:

'Gauti Tofason went with five warships out of the Gotha river, and when he was lying at Eker Island there came five large Danish merchant ships there. Gauti and his men immediately took four of the great vessels, and made a great

right: *Buckets, ladles and other kitchen utensils from the Oseberg ship. The largest bucket is 49 cm (about 19 in.) high.*

A ceremonial axehead from Denmark, inlaid with silver. It is 16.5 cm (6.5 in.) long.

booty without the loss of a man; but the fifth vessel slipped out to sea, and sailed away. Gauti gave chase with one ship, and at first came nearer to them; but as the wind increased, the Danes got away. Then Gauti wanted to turn back; but a storm came on, so that he lost his ship at Lesö, with all the goods, and the greater part of his crew. In the meantime his people were waiting for him at Eker; but the Danes came over in fifteen merchant ships, killed them all, and took all the booty they had made.'

The story is typical in its tough matter-of-fact reporting of robbery and death as if they were commonplace facts of life among Viking people. There are, however, some details which may seem less typical. This incident happened in 1020, and the ships were specialised: the Vikings were in longships, the merchants in knorrs, and a knorr proved a better sailer than a longship in bad weather. By now, too, the merchants were sailing in convoy for protection, and their fellow-countrymen were ready and able to take vengeance on the Vikings. It sounds as though by 1020 even a strong squadron of warships could easily come to grief on a raid, and the days when anyone could simply board his ship and set off on a Viking cruise were over.

The Vikings in western Europe

It was shortly before 800 that the first Viking raids hit the coasts of western Europe. At first they were small – just two or three ships which found themselves, almost by accident, near an easy target like the monastery of Lindisfarne. But the Angles and Saxons, Picts, Scots, Irish and Franks, even the Arabs in Spain, proved incapable of dealing with swift attacks from the sea: they simply did not possess anything to match the Viking ships, which gave the Vikings the huge advantage of being able to move quickly and, often, secretly. So it was not long before they were raiding in their hundreds.

The first large Viking fleets came to England about 835 and their tactic was to land and occupy an island, preferably in a river mouth, and build a permanent camp. They could then raid inland, using the ships to carry them up the rivers to new camps, and then taking horses to raid farther afield. This was where the Viking ship was shown to its fullest advantage. It could be quickly pulled on and off the shore and its draught was shallow enough to allow it to move up rivers. Sometimes the crews could moor their ships in midstream, and sleep under the sail draped as a tent over the deck. (Obviously, when navigating a winding river, the ship would be easiest to handle if oars were used and the mast lowered.) Sometimes they lodged their ships in specially dug berths in their camps.

The Viking camps were quite safe on the Isles of Sheppey and Thanet in England and on the islands on the River Seine in France. Local rulers became desperate and it was in this period that we first hear of a king of France paying money to the Vikings to stop them from pillaging. In modern language, it was 'protection money'. But they always came back and asked for more. A Dane, called Weland, offered the king of France 200 ships to fight the king of Denmark for a price. The price was too high and the offer was not accepted but the story shows that there was no loyalty among the Vikings unless it had been personally sworn. Weland must have been sure that the men in the 200 ships would follow him into battle against the king of their own country.

Meanwhile, in the Viking homelands, kings were gradually becoming more powerful. Often they were able to force Vikings to obey them, and often they themselves went on expeditions which were in most respects the biggest Viking raids of all. At about the time of the Skuldelev ships, England was attacked by several powerful fleets, and Viking commanders could still find new ways of using their longships. There is a remarkable story of a battle at London Bridge about 1010 which tells of protected ships:

'Olaf Haraldsson (St Olaf) ordered great platforms of floating wood to be tied together with hazel bands, and for this he broke up wattle huts; and with these, as a roof, he covered over his ships so widely, that it reached over the ships' sides. Under this screen he set pillars so high and stout, that there was room for swinging swords, and the roofs were strong enough to withstand the stones cast down upon them. Now when the fleet and men were ready, they rowed up along the river; but when they came near the bridge, there was cast down upon them so many stones and missile weapons, such as arrows and spears, that neither helmet nor shield could hold out against it; and the ships themselves were so greatly damaged that many retreated out of it. But Olaf and the fleet with him, rowed quite up under the bridge, laid their cables around the piles which supported it, and then rowed off with all their ships as hard as they could down the stream. The piles were thus shaken at the bottom, and were loosened under the bridge... Now as armed troops stood thick of men upon the bridge, and there was likewise many heaps of stone and other weapons upon it, and the piles under it being loosened and broken, the bridge gave way; and a great part of the men upon it fell into the river, and all the others fled, some into the castle, some into Southwark.'

Eventually, for a time, Danish kings ruled England. More important in the long run, Danes and Norwegians settled in many parts of England, Scotland and Ireland, and in northern France where the name of the Northmen is still preserved in Normandy.

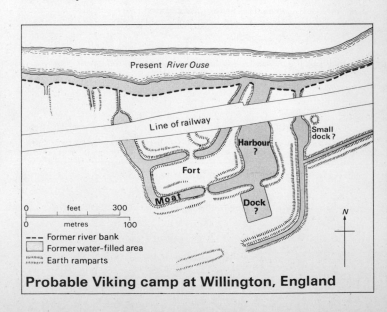

Probable Viking camp at Willington, England

The Vikings in eastern Europe

We have seen how their ships carried the Vikings, for trading and raiding, around the coast of Scandinavia: how they spread, doing the same sort of thing, to the other countries of western Europe, where they became conquerors and settlers in many areas: how they ventured further west and north, settling in the islands of the north Atlantic and even reaching North America. To the east there was less open sea; but there were rivers.

Most of the Vikings who came to Britain and France came from Denmark and Norway, and these two countries provided most of the colonists who sailed to Iceland. The Swedes also joined Danish and Norwegian crews, but their main sphere of interest was the Baltic Sea and the rivers flowing into it from Russia. That country gets its name because the Swedes were called the Rus folk, so their land became Rusland.

The Rus folk would find their voyages across the Baltic very similar to voyages in the North Sea but, once they reached the rivers, life would become very different from that in ships in other places. In the first place, there would be a lot of hard rowing against the currents. Most of the route was through silent forests. On wide stretches of the river, the wind could be strong at times as it blew along the channel between the trees, but the narrow stretches, where rapids were most likely to be found, would often be sheltered and windless. Rowing in such places in summer was extremely hot and tiring work. Insects, particularly mosquitoes, would pester the rowers.

The river traveller would have to be constantly on his guard, watching for pirates who could be lurking round every bend and in every inlet. Whereas the deep-sea sailor would usually see an enemy approaching from a distant horizon, any attack here would be very sudden. As the pirates were themselves Swedes, the greatest danger was encountered on the first part of the journey. Perhaps the ships sometimes went in fleets for mutual protection. The rivers were well used, so a ship would not have to wait for long for other ships to join it. It would have been risky, though, to assume that another merchant ship which happened to arrive while you were fighting pirates would come to your assistance; the crew might think it more profitable to help the pirates.

Piracy was often risky because ships on the rivers would carry large crews of fit men. These crews were needed not only for the

The plan on the left shows earthworks by the River Ouse in Bedfordshire which, it is suggested, are the remains of a Viking camp and harbour. The map on the right shows routes regularly used by Viking traders.

Viking trade routes
during the 10th and 11th centuries
- - - Trade routes
///// Settlements overseas

0   500 miles
0   1000 km

heavy rowing, but also for hauling the ship and cargo out of the water and onto logs, and dragging them along the river bank past rapids. The really heavy work came on those ships that had to be dragged across country from the smaller rivers to the headwaters of the Volga and Dnieper. This long haul could last more than a day, but everyone would hope to find a defensible position for the night. It would not be pleasant to be attacked while dragging a ship through a forest, and a night attack would even be worse.

Once they were past the portages, as such overland hauls are called, the crews would be travelling with the flow of the river and they would not be called upon to use much muscle power. But as they left the forest and sailed through the steppes, they encountered nomadic tribes who often attacked the Rus, and this was the most dangerous part of the journey. One tribe, the Pechenegs, eventually managed to close the Dnieper route by their persistent attacks on ships, especially at portages past rapids.

After weeks of danger, the Rus would bring their ships at last into the open waters of the Black Sea or the Caspian. Here they would trade with local merchants, Byzantines or Arabs perhaps, load their ships with fine eastern textiles, jewels and coins, and then face the long, hard journey home.

Sometimes they settled on the way, and around their towns (which grew into cities like Kiev), there arose powerful principalities which eventually became Russia. Sometimes they thought to gain more by pillage than trade. Making alliances with nearby tribes, they even sailed across the Black Sea to attack Constantinople, which they called Micklegarth, the great city. But not even the Viking ships could resist the famous Greek fire, a chemical mixture that burned when it came in contact with water.

The battle of Svoldr

As kings – and sometimes great jarls – became more powerful in the Viking homelands, often, no doubt, with wealth that had come from trade and fighting, they built more and bigger warships. We have already met *Long Serpent*, the greatest of them all. As it happens, there is a detailed account in one of the sagas of her last fight. It shows us how, by this time, the Vikings had developed their ideas of how to fight at sea, and explains why big war-galleys, useless for anything else, were very useful indeed in great battles.

King Olaf Tryggvason of Norway sailed into a trap with only seventy ships at Svoldr in AD 1000. He was aboard *Long Serpent* and he also had with him *Crane* and *Short Serpent* which were famed as being exceptionally large ships. But King Swein Forkbeard of Denmark had allied with King Olof of Sweden and Earl Eric of Norway to make a fleet large enough to defeat Olaf Tryggvason. This saga tells what happened when King Olaf sighted his enemies:

'King Olaf ordered the war horns to sound for all his ships to close up to each other. The king's ship lay in the middle of the line, and on one side lay *Short Serpent*, and on the other *Crane*; and as they made fast the stems together, the *Long Serpent*'s stem and the *Short Serpent*'s stem were made fast together; but when the king saw it he called out to his men and ordered them to lay the longer ship more in advance, so that its stern should not lie so far behind the fleet.

Then says Ulf the Red, "If the *Long Serpent* is to lie as much ahead of the other ships as she is longer than them, we shall have hard work of it here on the prow."

The king replies, "I did not think I had a man afraid as well as red." . . .

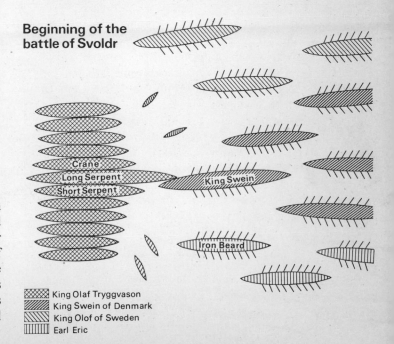

Beginning of the battle of Svoldr

Crane
Long Serpent
Short Serpent
King Swein
Iron Beard

King Olaf Tryggvason
King Swein of Denmark
King Olof of Sweden
Earl Eric

The kings then laid out their oars and prepared to attack. King Swein laid his ship against the *Long Serpent*. Outside of him Olof the Swede laid himself, and set his stem against the outermost ship of King Olaf's line; and on the other side lay Earl Eric. Then a hard combat began . . .

This battle was one of the severest told of, and many were the people slain. The prow men of *Long Serpent*, *Short Serpent*, and *Crane* threw grapplings and anchors into King Swein's ship, and used their weapons well against the people standing below them, for they cleared the decks of all the ships they could lay fast hold of; and King Swein, and all the men who escaped, fled to other vessels, and laid themselves out of bow-shot . . . But Earl Eric laid the *Iron Beard* side by side with the outermost of King Olaf's ships, thinned it of men, cut the cables, and let it drift. Then he laid alongside the next, and fought until he had cleared it of men also. Now all the people who were in the smaller ships began to run into the larger, and the earl cut them loose as fast as he cleared them of men. The Danes and Swedes laid themselves now within shooting distance all around Olaf's ship; but Earl Eric always lay close alongside of the ships, and used his swords and battle axes, and as fast as people fell in his vessel others, Danes and Swedes, came in their place . . .

Then the fight became most severe, and many people fell. But at last it came to this, that all of King Olaf Tryggvason's ships were cleared of men except *Long Serpent*, on board of which all who could still carry their arms were gathered. Then *Iron Beard* lay side by side with the *Serpent*, and the fight went on with battle axe and sword . . .

Earl Eric was in the stern of his ship where a cover of shields had been set up . . . So many weapons were cast into the *Serpent*, and so thick flew spears and arrows, that the shields could scarcely receive them; for on all sides the *Serpent* was surrounded by war ships. Then King Olaf's men became so mad with rage, that they ran on board of the enemies' ships, to get at the people with stroke of sword and kill them; but . . . most of Olaf's men went overboard and sank under their weapons, thinking they were fighting on plain ground . . .

Einar Thambarskelfir, one of the sharpest of bow shooters, stood by the mast, and shot with his bow. Einar shot an arrow at Earl Eric, which hit the tiller end just above the earl's head so hard that it entered the wood up to the arrowshaft . . . Then said the earl to a man called Finn, "Shoot that tall man by the mast." Finn shot; and the arrow hit the middle of Einar's bow just at the moment when Einar was drawing it, and the bow split into two parts.

"What is that," cried King Olaf, "that broke with such a noise?"

"Norway, king from thy hands," cried Einar.

"No! not quite so much as that," says the king; "take my bow, and shoot," flinging the bow at him.

Einar took the bow, and drew it over the head of the arrow.

"Too weak, too weak," said he, "for the bow of a mighty king!" and, throwing the bow back to him, he took sword and shield and fought.

The king stood on the beams of the *Long Serpent*, and shot the greater part of the day; sometimes with the bow, sometimes with the spear, and always throwing two spears at once. He looked down over the ship's side, and saw that his men struck briskly with their swords, and yet but wounded seldom. Then he called out, "Why do you strike so gently that ye seldom cut?" One among the people answered, "The swords are blunt and full of notches." Then the king went down into the stern, and opened the chest, and took out many sharp swords, which he handed to his men; but as he stretched out his right hand with them, some observed that blood was running down under his steel glove, but no one knew where he was wounded . . .

Now the fight became hot indeed, and many men fell on board the *Serpent*; and the men on board of her began to be thinned off, and the defence to be weaker. The earl resolved to board the *Serpent*, . . . and the earl's men poured in all around the vessel, and all the men who were still able to defend the ship crowded aft to the king, and arrayed themselves for his defence . . .

Few were the people left in the *Serpent* for defence against so great a force; and in a short time most of the *Serpent*'s men fell, brave and stout though they were. King Olaf sprang overboard on his own side of the ship; but the earl's men had laid out boats around the *Serpent*, and killed those who leapt overboard. Now when the king had leapt overboard, they tried to seize him with their hands, and bring him to Earl Eric; but King Olaf threw his shield over his head, and sank beneath the waters.'

This story shows how loyal the men could be to their leader and how honour could be gained by being the last one to remain fighting. But there are six main points to be noticed about this, the most famous of Viking sea battles.

First, the defenders formed an 'island' by fastening all their ships tightly alongside each other with the strongest in the centre of the line.

Second, the attackers tried to keep the centre occupied with spears and arrows while the weaker ships in the defence were boarded and cleared and cut adrift. This did not work perfectly because the men on the *Long Serpent* were able to get anchors aboard the attackers and drag them in for combat at close quarters.

Third, while Olaf's smaller ships were cleared, Earl Eric was sheltering behind the shield wall formed by his most trusted men as he would have done in a land battle. Any men that he lost during these preliminaries were replaced by others coming aboard from smaller ships. Eric and his men were waiting for the tough work of attacking the strongest ship in the defence.

Fourth, smaller boats, probably ships' rowing boats, swarmed round the main battle to catch anyone who tried to escape overboard.

Fifth, although the ships had masts, both attackers and defenders were rowed to battle positions. Wind could not be relied on to take ships within arrow distance but out of range of grappling hooks, and then to bring them to a full stop in exactly these positions. Sailors wrestling with a sail would make an easy target for enemy marksmen and they would impede their own warriors on the deck.

Sixth, although the sails do not appear to have been used, the masts were kept standing, presumably because they would have cluttered the deck if they had been lowered, and the sails might have been needed if the defenders had decided to try to escape from the battle.

This was the greatest of Viking sea battles. Never before, in northern European waters, had so many ships fought together, and it was to be centuries before there were any more great battles at sea involving any European nations.

The helmet from southern Sweden and the sword from Norway (it is about 93 cm (3 ft) long) both belong to a time just before the Vikings. They show the same love of ornamentation.

9 The descendants of the Viking ship

Changes very rarely come suddenly in history. An Englishman could be forgiven for thinking that, after their defeat at Stamford Bridge in 1066, the Vikings never attacked England again. History books often ignore later raids, but they did occur. The last recorded raid on north-east England was in 1151, and the Scots had their last battle with the Norwegians in 1263. So the Vikings were only slowly forgotten in Britain.

Their ships were also slowly modified until their original design was forgotten in the lands where they had raided and settled. This was a very gradual process and it was even more so in Scandinavia. Some of the sailing boats which operated out of north Norwegian ports at the beginning of this century looked very like Viking ships, and modern Scandinavian rowing boats often have the recognisable shape of a Viking hull.

It is therefore impossible to say that the last Viking ship was built in any particular year. And it is impossible to say that the process of modifying the design began at any particular time because, as we have already seen, there was never a standard design. Over a long period there was a tendency for fighting ships to carry more men and cargo ships to carry more cargo. Viking ships had been famous for their speed and manoeuvrability but some of these qualities were lost as they became bulkier.

Ships with valuable cargoes had to be made capable of defending themselves. If the sides of the vessel were heightened, then she would both be more difficult to board and have greater cargo-carrying capacity. But extra weight would make her lie lower in the water and so the ship, while losing some of the extra height, would not ride the waves so easily. Heightening the sides would also cause added difficulties in strong side winds, especially if the ship was lightly loaded.

Despite the disadvantages, the high-sided ships became more common. There was a demand for Scandinavian dried fish in Germany, and the Scandinavians wanted luxuries such as wine. So trade increased and cargoes became heavier. The German

Eleventh century: *The Bayeux Tapestry shows William the Conqueror using ships just like those of the Vikings.*

Twelfth century: *The font of Winchester Cathedral, about 1180, has a carving of a ship with a stern rudder, the first in northern Europe.*

Thirteenth century: *The seal of the port of Winchelsea shows a warship with high prow and stern and side rudder, with castles fore and aft to carry armed men.*
Fourteenth century: *The seal of Stralsund, 1329, shows the new type of ship used in north Germany, the cog, with straight stem and stern posts.*

Hanseatic ports slowly gained a monopoly of the trade but their ships, called cogs, had evolved from the general northern European design of double ended, clinker built ships with a single square sail. The first major change came with the introduction of the stern rudder, which was better suited to heavy deep-draughted vessels. The illustrations we have of this period show that the stern post was sometimes made straight to hang the rudder better. Even with a rounded stern though, a cog could never be likened to a snake.

Ships at this time were also being fitted with platforms at high points such as the bow, stern and masthead. Bowmen could stand on these platforms while they defended their ship. The sides of the platforms were castellated for added protection and so the word forecastle came into sailor's language.

Heavier cargoes also caused the introduction of carvel planking instead of clinker. The overlapping of the clinker planks meant that they could not be very thick, but there was no such limit to the carvel planks. Remains of a flat-bottomed ship of the thirteenth or fourteenth century were found in Kolding Fiord with the bottom carvel- and the sides clinker-built. We do not know when the first completely carvel ship appeared in northern Europe, but it seems likely to have been in the first part of the fifteenth century. Such ships could endure more weight and strain and therefore take larger and heavier masts. The bigger ships that could now be built could carry more, and profitable voyages could then be longer. It therefore became easier to trade across oceans and colonise newly discovered continents.

But the driving force in the great age of discovery did not come from Scandinavia. In 1523, when the Bishop of Bergen wanted a ship, he had to have it built in Holland as there was nobody on his own coast capable of building it. In the following year, a Danish ship had to put into Oslo for repairs. However, there were no carpenters or ships' parts available.

If the Viking tradition had long been forgotten in southern Norway, this was not true in the north where the land was so rough and mountainous that the people have always had to rely on the sea for their food and transport. Here boatbuilders retained the old skills. The same is true on the Atlantic islands where people had to have boats. The boatbuilder of the Faroes follows the Viking design; the Shetlanders remember their ancestors in a more light-hearted way, building a replica longship every year and burning it in the Up-Hellya ceremony.

right: *A modern boat builder's shed in the Faroe Islands. Even today the hull shape discovered by the Vikings a thousand years ago cannot be bettered.*

Replica Viking ships have been built at various places in Denmark, by scouts and other organisations. A number of these have sailed across the North Sea and one of these, the *Hugin*, can be seen on the seafront at Ramsgate.

The original Gokstad ship is in a specially built museum in Oslo along with the beautifully carved Oseberg ship and the smaller Tune ship. These are still the best-preserved original Viking ships in existence. There is also a special ship museum at Roskilde in Denmark for the remains of the Skuldelev ships. Though the visitor to Roskilde will only see the remains of ships' timbers and not complete ships, he will also be able to appreciate the painstaking care, the scientific knowledge and the expense that have gone into preserving these pieces of wood. They were worth preserving, not only as reminders of a heroic age, but as some of the most beautiful and efficient instruments ever made by man.

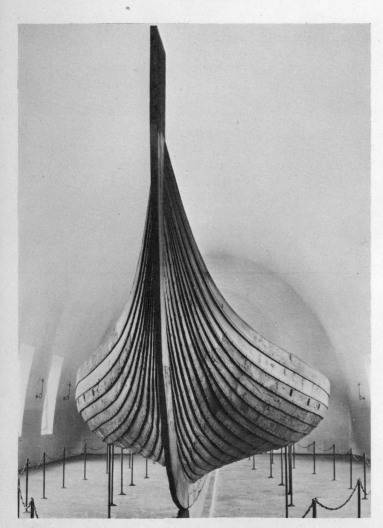

This modern copy of a Viking ship, called 'Hugin', was built in Denmark and sailed across the North Sea in 1949; it is now displayed near Ramsgate.

The Gokstad ship today, in the Ship Museum at Oslo.

The five Skuldelev wrecks in the Roskilde Museum.

Index

Acknowledgments

The author and publisher would like to thank the following for permission to reproduce illustrations:
pp.1, 25 (right), 46 (above) National Maritime Museum, London; pp.2, 36 (amulet and necklace), 44 (helmet) Museum of National Antiquities, Stockholm. Photographs ATA; pp.9, 13, 14, 18, 26, 36 (sledge and cart), 37 (buckets), 44 (sword hilt), 48 (Gokstad ship) University Museum of National Antiquities, Oslo; pp.20, 21, 22, 48 (below right) The Viking Ship Museum, Roskilde, Denmark; p.29 National Museum of Antiquities of Scotland; pp.30, 31, 45 (above) Phaidon Press Ltd. Photographs Victoria and Albert Museum; pp.37 (axehead), 47 (above) National Museum, Copenhagen. Photographs Lennart Larsen; p.45 (below) Royal Commission on Historical Monuments, Crown Copyright; p.46 (below) State Archive, Hamburg; p.47 (below) Royal Danish Embassy; p.48 (top right) Thanet District Council; back cover J. Combier, Mâcon, France.

The drawings on pp.1, 24, 25 (right), 27 are reproduced with grateful acknowledgement to O. Crumlin-Pedersen of The Viking Ship Museum, Roskilde.

The extracts from the sagas on pp.30, 35, 36, 38, 41, 42 were translated by Samuel Laing and published in Snorri Sturluson (ed.), *Heimskringla* parts 1 and 2, Dent Everyman, 1964, 1961. The extract on p.34 is from B. Almgren (ed.), *The Viking*, C. A. Watts, 1966, which also provides much valuable information about many aspects of the Viking way of life.

Reconstruction drawings, maps and diagrams by Keith Howard, Leslie Marshall and Reg Piggott
Front cover painting by David Bryant

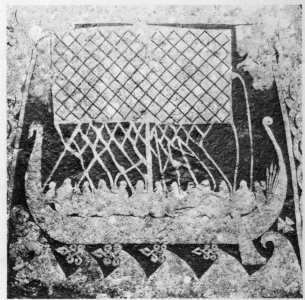

A carved and painted stone from the Swedish island of Gotland showing a Viking ship at sea. It is 3 m (10 ft) high.

Front cover: *The Gokstad ship as it may have appeared in the ninth century.*

Back cover: *A scene from the Bayeux Tapestry, made soon after 1066, shows shipbuilders at work.*

The Cambridge History Library

The Cambridge Introduction to History
Written by Trevor Cairns

PEOPLE BECOME CIVILIZED   EUROPE AND THE WORLD

THE ROMANS AND THEIR EMPIRE   THE BIRTH OF MODERN EUROPE

BARBARIANS, CHRISTIANS, AND MUSLIMS   THE OLD REGIME AND THE REVOLUTION

THE MIDDLE AGES   POWER FOR THE PEOPLE

The Cambridge Topic Books
General Editor Trevor Cairns

THE AMERICAN WAR OF INDEPENDENCE
by R. E. Evans

BENIN: AN AFRICAN KINGDOM AND CULTURE
by Kit Elliott

THE BUDDHA
by F. W. Rawding

BUILDING THE MEDIEVAL CATHEDRALS
by Percy Watson

THE EARLIEST FARMERS AND THE FIRST CITIES
by Charles Higham

EARLY CHINA AND THE WALL
by P. H. Nancarrow

THE FIRST SHIPS AROUND THE WORLD
by W. D. Brownlee

HERNAN CORTES: CONQUISTADOR IN MEXICO
by John Wilkes

LIFE IN A FIFTEENTH-CENTURY MONASTERY
by Anne Boyd

LIFE IN THE IRON AGE
by Peter J. Reynolds

LIFE IN THE OLD STONE AGE
by Charles Higham

MARTIN LUTHER
by Judith O'Neill

MEIJI JAPAN
by Harold Bolitho

THE MURDER OF ARCHBISHOP THOMAS
by Tom Corfe

MUSLIM SPAIN
by Duncan Townson

POMPEII
by Ian Andrews

THE PYRAMIDS
by John Weeks

THE ROMAN ARMY
by John Wilkes

ST. PATRICK AND IRISH CHRISTIANITY
by Tom Corfe

THE VIKING SHIPS
by Ian Atkinson

The Cambridge History Library will be expanded in the future to include additional volumes. Lerner Publications Company is pleased to participate in making this excellent series of books available to a wide audience of readers.